To Beverley Nichols
from us both

The Ambrose Rock

DEREK TANGYE

Illustrated by Jean Tangye

SPHERE BOOKS LIMITED
London and Sydney

First published in Great Britain by
Michael Joseph Ltd 1982
Copyright © 1982 by Derek Tangye
Published by Sphere Books Ltd 1983
30–32 Gray's Inn Road, London WC1X 8JL
Reprinted 1985

Set in Garamond

Printed and bound in Great Britain by
Cox & Wyman Ltd, Reading

THE AMBROSE ROCK

Derek Tangye has become famous all over the world for his series of bestsellers about his flower farm in Cornwall. The series, which began with *A Gull on the Roof*, describes a simple way of life which thousands of his readers would like to adopt themselves.

Derek and his wife left their glamorous existence in London when they discovered Minack, a deserted cottage close to the cliffs of Mount's Bay. Jeannie gave up her job as Press Relations Officer of the Savoy Hotel Group and Derek Tangye resigned from MI5. They then proceeded to carve from the wild land around the cottage the meadows which became their flower farm.

Derek Tangye's bestsellers include *Cottage on a Cliff, A Cat Affair* and *The Way to Minack*.

Also by Derek Tangye in Sphere Books:

THE WAY TO MINACK
COTTAGE ON A CLIFF
SUN ON THE LINTEL
A CAT AFFAIR
SOMEWHERE A CAT IS WAITING
LAMA
A DONKEY IN THE MEADOW
THE WINDING LANE
WHEN THE WINDS BLOW
A CAT IN THE WINDOW
A CORNISH SUMMER
A DRAKE AT THE DOOR
A GULL ON THE ROOF

The Ambrose Rock

ONE

Ambrose followed me into the cottage out of the rain, a wet ginger sponge; and walked over to the space beneath my desk, and began to lick the wet away.

'Come over here,' I said, sitting down on the sofa; 'let me dry you.'

He ignored me.

'Come on, Ambrose ...'

He continued to lick.

'Come on ...'

Jeannie appeared from the tiny kitchen.

'Won't you ever learn,' she said, 'that you can never persuade a cat to do anything it doesn't want to do?'

'I was wanting to make a fuss of him.'

'I understand.'

It was early March and the daffodil season was at its height, and I had just returned from taking the daffodil boxes to Penzance Station en route to Covent Garden. The last sending of the week, for it was Friday afternoon.

'Many going away?' asked Jeannie.

'Too many. Tomlin's lorry was ahead of me, and Le Grice's horsebox, and the lorry from that huge Manaccan grower whose name I can never remember ... I should think the market will be swamped.'

'Anyhow, it's Friday, and we can have a rest.'

I sat in the corner of the sofa, sipping my tea. The sofa is on the right as you come into the cottage from the porch, standing between the door and the rough stone wall beside the fireplace; a high-backed sofa, high enough to lean your head against the top of it as you sit; a Victorian sofa, a

1

comfortable sofa, a sofa which I first knew years, years ago when I was a schoolboy at Harrow.

Its home, at that time, was a small Regency house called Rutlands, which was set in a rambling garden at Bushey Heath twenty miles from London, off a narrow road called The Ruts. My aunt lived there before her marriage, and she shared the house with an old friend of our family whom my aunt and my mother had known since they were children, and who had been bridesmaid at my mother's wedding. She was called by all of us ... Gar.

As a child, I never questioned the reason for this curious name. I took it for granted; just as I took it for granted that Gar, though unrelated, was a matriarch of the family; and that major decisions should receive her approval, or a new girl friend should be quickly introduced to her. Over the years, I introduced a succession of such girl friends until finally there was Jeannie.

Gar was a large lady with wisps of hair on her chin, who dressed in sombre-coloured clothes, and who was always elderly as far as I was concerned. She had a comfortable private income but, instead of sitting back and idly enjoying it in the genteel manner of those days, she was a very active, unpaid social worker. She was very generous to me and my two brothers, and particularly generous to my eldest brother who was her godson; but my own special memory of her was her wonderful capacity to listen. If I had some excitement in my life I wanted to share, I would know that Gar would be there to share it; and during the years of growing up, I was to spend hours talking to her and, whether or not she was interested in my outpourings, she always appeared to be interested. I was to discover, however, a warning sign when I had embarked on a topic of which she disapproved. She would sit in the corner of the sofa, which is now my own favourite corner … and gently begin to sway backwards and forwards.

Gar, my aunt, and Rutlands seemed to be a safe, indestructible world; and it never dawned on me that my presence could ever have been a nuisance to them. Life seemed to be too well ordered for there to be nuisances. Breakfast, morning coffee, during which my aunt would be sitting in one corner of the sofa (the back faced the French windows opening out onto the garden) reading the *Daily Mail*, Gar in the other corner reading *The Times*; then followed lunch, tea, dinner, prepared and served by Betty the housekeeper or her daughter Bobbie. It never occurred to me in those youthful days that the world could ever be turned upside down.

Nor, for that matter, did it ever occur to me that I, Derek, could ever possibly be guilty of turning the world of Rutlands upside down. I had a child's innocence to believe that I was always welcome, never doubting the affection that Gar and my aunt always showed me, never realising that such affection could sometimes be severely tested.

My mother and father, during my Harrow days, spent much of their time in Germany, where my father had a senior position in British Intelligence. Their absence from England resulted, from time to time, in the puzzle as to what to do with Derek at half-term; or where he could stay when he was about to go to Germany, or when he had returned; and later there was the most serious problem of all ... who was to care for Derek during the Eton and Harrow match at Lords?

I fancy that my end of term visits to Rutlands and the pre-beginning of term visits were only minor irritations, passing moments of froth that trivially disturbed the Rutlands routine. The Eton and Harrow match at Lords, however, was very different. Prestige was at stake. All through the summer term my fellow pupils would discuss which shows they would be asking their parents to take them to, what nightclubs they might with daredevilry visit, what sisters of friends they might escort, and what waistcoats to wear. Waistcoats were very important, fawn, grey, even a modest pink, and they always had to be double-breasted, a black morning coat half hiding them.

Gar and my aunt, having been cajoled by my parents to do so, had therefore to leave the steady world of Rutlands for an excursion into this peacock world of Harrovians and Etonians, and for two days and two evenings, Friday and Saturday, cater for those social requirements which would help me to compete with the boasting of my fellow Harrovians when I returned to the school on the Monday.

They never failed me. Weeks in advance they would write and ask me what shows I would like to see. Then, nearer the time, they would send me the money to buy the tickets for lobster lunches and strawberry cream teas at the Harrow Tent; and in due course they would accompany me to Lords and we would enjoy the lobster lunches and strawberry cream teas, and I would watch the cricket, and they would find deck-chairs to sit upon, watching the passers-by in their finery; passers-by who had no interest in the cricket, who were only present to be part of the social scene. It never occurred to me that Gar and my aunt might not be interested in the social scene, and that they were only waiting patiently for the next stage of my entertainment.

At half past six, when stumps were drawn, we took a bus to Piccadilly Circus and walked to Mrs Brown's in Wardour Street. Mrs Brown's, unlike the reputation of the street, was the epitome of a respectable, small restaurant which catered for clients like Gar and my aunt, middle class people who, on a shopping or theatre visit to the West End, had a reliable place to go, either to recover from their shopping expedition, or to prepare for a theatre visit. My own memory of Mrs Brown's is of shiny wooden tables, the ample-bosomed Mrs Brown herself, well-bred waitresses and very small helpings.

Thus, when the three of us left Mrs Brown's on our way to the London Hippodrome or His Majesty's, or at whichever theatre the show of my choice was playing, I was already looking forward to the special treat of after-theatre supper at the Trocadero, which stood off Shaftesbury Avenue close to Piccadilly Circus. At the show, of course, there were the chocolates, bought by Gar from the tray of a pretty attendant, but it was the prospect of the Trocadero that kept welling up in my mind as I ate the chocolates and enjoyed the show.

Unfortunately, the treat had always to be taken in a hurry. We would be escorted to a table, Gar and my aunt now both very weary, where I would order a rump steak, Béarnaise sauce, peas and new potatoes, followed by a Knickerbocker Glory ice-cream and marshmallow sauce. I had to gobble it. Only three-quarters of an hour could be spared for my treat. At 11.15 p.m. the last Greenline bus left the Piccadilly Circus end of Regent Street for Bushey Heath.

The journey, I remember, gave a chance for Gar and my aunt to nod, doze and sleep. I, too, was tired but the journey for me was filled with the excitements of the day. Jack Buchanan at the show had been romantically charming, and there was the kaleidoscope of people I had met at Lords to sort out in my mind. Only at the Greenline journey's end did I suddenly realise I too was very tired.

The bus drew up not far from The Ruts, a street lamp lighting up the stop. Then, leaving it behind, the three of us walked in the darkness, silently, and turned into the gateway of Rutlands, and Gar fumbled for the key, and we were through the door, and the light of the sitting room was switched on and there was the sofa, and I flopped down on it. A wonderful day. Tomorrow would be another wonderful day. I never thought that Gar and my aunt might think otherwise.

Fortunately for them, the year came when I announced that I was no longer interested in following the conventional route to Lords, to the lobster lunches, to the shows; and that instead I would make use of the weekend to dash to Cornwall, to our Glendorgal home at Porth near Newquay. I stayed there on my own, a fleeting visit, down by the Cornish Riviera on Friday, back by the night train on Sunday, but it was worth it. I gloried in walking along the beaches, climbing the rocks, feeling the wind brushing my face; but no exotic meals. I had once told the gardener's wife, who was cooking for me, how much I had enjoyed her shepherd's pie. I thereupon was given shepherd's pie on Friday evening, on Saturday evening, and I only just stopped her giving it me again before I left for London on Sunday.

Gar and my aunt were dog people and, during this period of my life, when staying at Rutlands I, who also was a dog person, often used to sit on the sofa with a dog at my feet. First there was an engaging Sealyham belonging to my aunt; and then came Simon, a soppy, willing-to-adore-anyone, golden labrador, much beloved by Gar. He would lay his head on my knee as I sat on the sofa, looking up at me adoringly, and I would take the adoring for granted. As a dog person, I knew that dogs loved the human race, trusting it, never believing that the human race could treat a dog cruelly. In due course, in the same corner of the sofa, I was to discover that cats viewed the human race less generously; or, more accurately, that cats were sceptical. A dog will trust any human who makes a friendly approach to it. A cat, I was to learn, is choosy.

My Harrow days were over and I became a clerk in Unilever. I had a room in a friend's house in Harrow, and then I matured into two rooms of my own at 38 Cranley Gardens, off the Brompton Road in Kensington, and my visits to the sofa at Rutlands became less and less frequent. Sometimes I have wondered what conversations about me took place on the sofa between Gar and my aunt. They both showed much affection towards me, but I have an irking feeling that they disapproved of me. I believe that there must have been occasions when Gar at one end of the sofa and my aunt at the other deplored the fact that I was not predictable. They were on guard against my maverick behaviour; suspicious of it. There was the occasion, after her marriage, that my aunt and her husband were staying at Glendorgal and they had decided to set off home, after their stay, at six in the morning. I planned a surprise for my aunt. I would be there to wave them goodbye, and this I did. Many years later, I reminded my aunt of the occasion, and I was startled by her reply. She thought that the reason why I had risen so early to see her off ... was my thankfulness to see her go. An example of how one's interpretation of another person's behaviour can often be so wrong.

Gar sold Rutlands after my aunt's marriage, and came to live in London, at 42 Jubilee Place in Chelsea, off the Kings Road. The sofa did not go with her. The sofa, she decided, was unsuitable for the small square room which was to become her drawing room, and she was about to sell it when my mother, always anxious not to miss any opportunities that would benefit her sons, persuaded her otherwise. I had spent two years as a newspaper reporter in Manchester, and had now returned to London to work on a London newspaper, and was about to move into a Chelsea flat, a mews cottage in fact, and my mother was gathering furniture for it like a squirrel gathering nuts for its winter nest. Thus Gar, at my

7

mother's gentle suggestion, did not sell the sofa, but generously gave it to me instead.

Sofas, such as this sofa, are the subject of much heaving and lifting and manipulating, as they move from old homes to new homes; and this sofa, this Rutlands sofa, proved to be particularly obstinate when the removal men tried to manoeuvre it into its appointed place in my mews cottage ... through the small door in Elm Park Garden Mews, as it was then called, up the narrow stairs into the sitting room, with no door separating stairs from room, then placed with the high back of the sofa against the rail of the staircase. I watched the removal men ecstatically. The first home of my own. The smell of fresh paint; the excitement of new furniture; a new carpet; new curtains; the prospect of youthful freedom, doing work I relished ... and the comfortable reassurance of a familiar sofa.

The sofa, however, no longer was part of a well-regulated existence and, instead, became the pivot of a turbulent bachelordom. There, in the corner where Gar or my aunt once sat, I would pour into my diary vivid accounts of my ecstasies and my miseries, scrawling my words as if I were in a booth confessing to a hidden priest, exorcising my emotions of guilt, inadequacy and foolish moments of brashness; and then, diary resting on my knees, I would dream of the life I wanted to lead, of the girl whom I would find one day, who was wandering around in some part of the world that very moment, who would become my wife. I was naive sitting on the sofa writing my diary. I was simple in the way I described sudden new love; sudden lost love.

Yet the exuberance of my youthful diary was to be of help to me in the years to come. The emotions I wrote about were to remain constant. Age did not change them, and when, as I grew older, I re-read my diary, I did not feel any wiser. I did not feel, because of age, that I could patronise youth. My own youth was still with me, in my diary, and the thrills and the miseries, the frustrations and the foolishness remained fresh. My imagination relives the scrawled passages in my diary as I sit in the corner of the sofa where, long ago, they were written. And there were the lessons I have learnt from my diary.

Missed opportunities are what one regrets as one grows older; opportunities missed by a momentary lack of boldness, or a fear of hurting someone's feelings, or because, when the opportunity came, one was blind to its value. I read in my diary of my own missed opportunities and realise they were usually due to a terror of making a fool of myself. If only I had been bolder! ... is the comment I read again and again. Yet there were opportunities I did not miss.

I progressed in my Fleet Street career, flitting from story to story, pursuing murderers, interviewing film stars, eating free in restaurants, reporting Churchill speeches warning of coming war. It was a merry, hectic period of my life, which became more hectic when suddenly I was plucked from the ranks of ordinary reporting into being a columnist on the *Daily Mirror*. Overnight I became a star. My youthful face peered down from the tops of buses in advertisements which shrieked READ DEREK TANGYE; and I would stand in Piccadilly, watching my face on a Number 22 rushing one way and on a Number 19 rushing the other way. I was courted by ambitious politicians, by the world of show business, by public relations officers who pressed upon me their wares. And then suddenly my stardom ended.

I was about to make a tour of the capitals of Europe, my suitcase packed, when I was called to the editor's office. 'We're changing our policy,' he said, 'you're fired.' I was top of the world one moment; at the bottom the next. Moreover, I realised that no other newspaper had a need for my kind of column, and so my inevitable future would lie in a return to being an ordinary reporter. It was now that I was faced with an opportunity that I did *not* miss.

After stiff drinks at El Vinos, the Fleet Street mecca, I returned to the office with an idea which came to me after my third stiff drink.

'May I,' I asked the editor, 'write one more column? ... I am going round the world!'

I returned to my mews cottage that evening, and sat down on the sofa with a pad of notepaper and drafted out the column. It was a graphic column giving a romantic picture of the places I hoped to visit, and giving no hint to my readers that I had been fired.

'There are some who will call me a fool for doing this,' I wrote with enthusiasm, 'but I don't think youth should let the desire for security cramp the spirit of adventure. When you are so young, you should have the courage to seize the best out of life, so that when you are old you can look back on the years and say: "I have lived." '

A couple of weeks later, I was off to America, and my brother rented my mews cottage ... a month in New York, a Greyhound bus to San Francisco; Hollywood, Panama, steerage to Tahiti, lolling in the South Seas, Fiji, New Zealand, Australia, Manila, Hong Kong, Shanghai, Japan, Manchuria, the Trans-Siberian Railway, Moscow, Warsaw, Berlin, Paris, and home to Britain, and the war. A year had passed.

The sofa went into storage soon after the war had started and survived in an Ealing-based warehouse until Jeannie and I were married and we moved into a house at Mortlake, a house with a roof like a dunce's cap and situated opposite the finishing post of the Boat Race. Jeannie was at the Savoy Hotel, the public relations officer coping with the world's war correspondents, and I was in MI5, innocently meeting KGB spies like Philby and Blunt.

We had been married three months and I was still a dog lover, a cat hater, when one afternoon I arrived in Jeannie's office at the Savoy and found a tiny ginger kitten the colour of autumn bracken playing with a typewritter ribbon on the carpet. I was at first suspicious, then indignant. Jeannie's mother had given her the kitten, and I was expected to take it home to Mortlake. My indignation was made clear: 'I'll throw it over Hammersmith Bridge as I pass,' I said.

The kitten became Monty, and I wrote the story of his life in *A Cat in the Window*, and I dedicated that book to Jeannie's mother. Thus, you see, I did not throw him over Hammersmith Bridge and, in the days that followed in Mortlake, he wooed me, and incident by incident he led me away from being a cat hater. The first of those incidents occurred on the sofa, on the high back of the sofa.

'I was alone in the top room,' I wrote in *A Cat in the Window*, 'when there was a noise at the door as if it were being kicked by a soft boot. I opened it and Monty came scampering in. He rushed to the sofa, jumped up, climbed on the back, walking along it tail up, then down again to the floor and across to where I was standing, arching his back, rubbing his head against my leg and purring.'

The moment when I was no longer a cat hater.

The sofa came to Minack when we moved from Mortlake and, because there was no lane down from the farm at the top of the hill, it was manhandled across the fields by four men, and placed against the wall on the right of the door, where it stands now. Within a few days, Monty, who had come with us to share our new life, had decided that his favourite corner on the sofa, where he was to spend countless hours curled up sleeping, was to be my own favourite corner. We competed for it. Just as I was to compete for it in the years to come after Monty died ... first with Lama, then with Oliver, then Ambrose.

I was standing by Monty's Leap, close to where Monty is buried, when I first saw Ambrose. Oliver who, like Lama, was all black, was courting us at the time, hovering around the environment of the cottage, denied acceptance by us because Lama was then the queen of Minack and, at any cost, her feelings were not to be hurt.

11

Oliver used to come across the fields from a farm over the hill, a mile or so away as the crow flies. He would stop at Monty's Leap, a black double of Lama, and Jeannie and I would wonder why it was that he would choose to come to Minack in all weathers when he had a comfortable home at the farm. There was, however, an explanation.

A little grey cat we called Daisy used to haunt the fields around Minack. She was very wild and we never were able to come near her till the last few days of her life, when we found her lying in the grass by the lane and we nursed her till she died. It was this Daisy, however, who offered the clue as to why Oliver had chosen to adopt us.

It was a September morning six years previous to the moment we first saw Oliver at Monty's Leap. We were planting daffodil bulbs in one of the meadows down the cliff. Suddenly Geoffrey, our help, shouted there was a tiny black kitten in the neighbouring meadow. It promptly disappeared; disappeared for the rest of the morning, and it was not until evening that Jeannie found it again, curled asleep on a patch of dry leaves in a tiny cave cut in the cliff. It ran away again.

During the following days, Jeannie left saucers of milk and food nearby to the cave, and we would hide behind a hedge and wait and watch. Daisy would appear, then the kitten. A week later, there was another development. I went into the old barn in front of the cottage ... and the kitten was curled asleep on a sack.

Of course, Jeannie again proceeded to feed it and she would leave the saucers on the cobbled floor, and then we would observe the kitten through the barn window. It was neat and compact, very much the shape of Lama, the chief difference being its tail. It was a very thin tail. And there was another special feature about the kitten. When it drank milk from the saucer, it splashed it all over its face. Ten days after I first saw it in the barn, it disappeared ... six years later came Oliver. He too had a very thin tail, had very much the shape of Lama, and splashed milk all over his face. When the kitten left the barn, did it find its way to the farm and join the farm cats? We believe it did. Oliver was the kitten, and now he had come back to where he was born. So there I was, one day, standing by Monty's Leap and watching Oliver, who was a few yards up the lane. I was just looking, thinking of nothing in particular, when suddenly I was startled by an astonishing sight...from out of the undergrowth at the side of the lane stumbled a tiny ginger kitten towards Oliver. I was amazed. It was uncanny. There, in front of me, was the double of Monty, a tiny ginger kitten the colour of autumn bracken. It was as if I were back again in Jeannie's office at the Savoy.

I reacted also in the same way as when I first saw Monty.

'Jeannie,' I said, 'we simply can't have another cat, so *please*, *please* don't feed it.'

Jeannie did not listen to me.

Oliver now had an ally, and this encouraged him to infiltrate further into the Minack surroundings. He was growing more confident, but the kitten ... the kitten, or Ambrose, as he was later to be called, was as unfriendly as a wild cat. It was impossible to get near to him. He was, however, devoted to Oliver, and Oliver proceeded to treat him with the same care and affection as a mother cat. The love between them was charming to watch. They hunted together and curled up together and, as Ambrose grew older, Oliver would take him on expeditions and we might not see either of them for a whole day. How strange it was for Jeannie and me. A black cat and a ginger cat, both uninvited, who were the doubles of Lama and Monty.

When Lama's reign at Minack was over, Oliver entered the cottage as if he owned it; the mission accomplished. The mission which had begun two years before when first we saw him close to Monty's Leap. Ambrose, on the other hand, showed little wish to be part of our home. He seemed to have an in-built distrust of the human race. He would run away if I approached him, or if Jeannie advanced towards him with a tempting saucer of fish. Only at night was he friendly, and that was when the lights were out, the window open, and Jeannie and I were in bed. Then, at some period in the night, we would wake up to hear a loud purring at the end of the bed. Ambrose had come in and was snuggling close to Oliver.

Five years had gone by and now, as I said at the beginning, Ambrose had followed me into the cottage out of the rain, a wet ginger sponge, and he had gone over to the space beneath my desk, and begun to lick the wet away.

'Come over here,' I had said, sitting down on the sofa, 'let me dry you.'

And he had ignored me.

I was wanting to make a fuss of him.

Oliver had died the day before.

TWO

The sun shone the following week, day after day.

'Lovely weather,' said the postman, as he drew up outside the cottage in his little red van.

'Lovely weather,' said the man at the garage, as he filled up the car with petrol.

Lovely weather, lovely weather ...

Not for us.

'Damn the sun,' I would murmur repeatedly during the course of the day. 'Damn the sun.'

The sun is no friend to the early daffodil grower. A mild, sunny March morning, everyone rejoicing that winter seems to be over, birds singing, romance in the air ... and the daffodil grower is frustrated.

'Don't go *on* so,' said Jeannie, cheerfully, on this particular morning. I saw her point. I had already damned the sun five times.

'It maddens me, though. It's warmer than the summer.'

'But you can't do anything about it.'

My frustration, my daffodil-growing frustration, was due to the sun bringing the daffodils on too fast. A Wordsworth field of daffodils may be pretty to look at, but commercially they are a total loss. Daffodils arriving in the market must be in tight bud, not a peep of yellow must be showing. Each bunch of ten must resemble a bunch of green pencils, so straight and upright must they be.

'I *can* do something about it,' I said.

'Yes?'

'Stop sending.'

Jeannie was silent. She was bunching at the bench in the small greenhouse, a collection of galvanised tins in front of her full of the California daffodils which we had picked before breakfast that morning. California, or Pentewan as they are sometimes called, have long stems, are a pale yellow and have deeper golden yellow centres. They also have a gentle scent, and are long lasting whether picked open or in bud. Nevertheless, the market still required them only in bud.

'Strange,' said Jeannie a moment later, still deftly bunching, gathering the stems from the tins, placing the completed bunch among the others beside her, ignoring what I had said to her, 'how impermanent is permanence.'

'What is the meaning of such a profound remark?' I teased.

'Well,' she said, 'Monty seemed permanent at the time; and Lama too; and Oliver ...'

'And open daffodils,' I added, bringing back the subject which was on my mind. Once upon a time, the market only wanted open daffodils.

'That's what I mean. There's no such thing as permanence.'

When we first came to Minack, no commercial daffodil grew on the land; no potato for that matter. It was rough, bracken-covered ground, spattered with huge boulders, much of it steep and falling like a mountain side down to the rocks and the sea. The grey stone cottage was derelict, the floor was of earth, there was no water except for a stream which dried up in summer, no electricity, of course; and so small was the space that, even now, we have only two rooms within the confines of the cottage walls. The windows were tiny, two looking out onto the little garden and the slope of the hill behind it; another three looking eastwards to the moorland on the other side of the valley and to the vastness of Mount's Bay and the shadowy line of the Lizard in the distance. Over the years, we were to stare out onto this moorland, wishing it were ours, sometimes scared by rumours that it was to be developed, knowing that if this were to happen our private world would be lost.

We rented the cottage and ten acres of the bracken-covered ground without even signing a formal document. Sensible people, had we asked their advice, would have warned us that, without a formal document, we had no security. We did not, however, choose to ask the advice of sensible people. Jeannie and I were at a stage in our lives when something inside ourselves, nothing logical, no long-term plan involved, was driving us to make a drastic change in our routine. We had grown tired of London's sophisticated insincerity. We wanted to find roots. We were in the mood of those who, weary of over-familiarity with their daily tasks, decide to emigrate. Except that I as a Cornishman, and Jeannie as a Celt, had no wish to emigrate further away than Cornwall.

In due course, the bracken-covered ground was broken into small fields, and into meadows that fell like stepping-stones down to the sea. It was a period of time when a peasant form of husbandry was still feasible. We had no need to be horticultural experts. Local farmers, generations of experience behind them, were our teachers, and the lessons they taught were simple ones ... have this variety of potato seed for the cliff meadows, a later variety for the small fields ... plant this distance between each row ... do not dig the crop until the bottom leaves are turning yellow. Our horticultural ignorance did not seem to matter. Scientific knowledge was unnecessary. Nature, aided by traditional methods, would ensure our prosperity. We did not bargain for the weather. We did not know, in the beginning, that the wind was to be our enemy.

Potatoes in the summer; daffodils in the spring. These were to be our main harvests, though we were also to grow violets, anemones, wallflowers and calendulas. The small flowers, coming out of seed packets, were cheap to grow. Daffodils, however, required capital; and therefore we considered ourselves lucky when an old friend of Jeannie's father, who had a flower farm in the Isles of Scilly, offered to sell us a large quantity of bulbs at well below the market price. Unfortunately, we were not then aware that there are fashions in daffodils and, although some varieties may remain in fashion over the years, there are many which do not. We spent many hours planting our bulbs from the Scillies; waited expectantly for the spring, and found they belonged to the latter group. Our time and money had been wasted.

When my mother died, she left a small legacy which was divided between myself and my two brothers. My father had died ten years before, and he and I had much in common. He used to take me on fly-fishing expeditions during school holidays, and we used regularly to fish the Fowey River near Bodmin Road station. We would park the car at the station, then dressed in waterproof trousers and boots, a rod in hand, a satchel hung over the back containing a compartment where the captured trout would be placed, and a little aluminium box containing the various flies we might use, we would walk a few hundred yards down the main road, turn left into an untidy timber yard, and then through a wooden field gate to the banks of the river. We would then separate. He would walk perhaps a quarter of a mile up the river, while I began to cast my line nearby to the gate. We shared the knowledge that the special pleasure of fly fishing lay in solitude.

My father was a successful barrister when he was young, but chose to remain in the British Army of the Rhine after the First World War as a senior Intelligence Officer. He held several public appointments when he retired. He was a Deputy Lieutenant of Cornwall; Chairman of the Cornwall Quarter Sessions and, during the Hitler war, he was Deputy Chief Constable in charge of the Special Constabulary. He was a rich man when he was young and a barrister, but his money whittled away as the years passed and, in the latter part of his life, he was consumed by financial worry. The worry centred, in particular, around Glendorgal, the old family home on the outskirts of Newquay. He loved Glendorgal and the land which belonged to it with a passion. The rambling house was poised above its own bay, and looked northwards up the rugged coast of Watergate Bay, Bedruthan Steps, and the island rocks of Trevose Head. My father used to judge the worth of my friends by their reactions to the beauty of Glendorgal. If they were muted in their admiration, he lost interest in them. In Jeannie's case, she passed the test. Jeannie saw Glendorgal just before my father died. Her enthusiasm for its wild beauty did not disappoint him.

My father and mother never failed to encourage me in my youthful hopes. When, for instance, I told my father I wanted to give up my job as a clerk in Unilever in order to try to become a journalist, he did not set out to dissuade me. He was a father who believed that a son should work out his own destiny if the son had a clear idea what he wanted to achieve. He was not going to interfere with me, though he may have doubted my wisdom.

I realise, of course, that my mother influenced him in my favour. My mother would argue on my behalf, and did so often when the arguments in my favour were thin. She would argue, too, with Gar and my aunt when they showed disapproval of some decision I had made. My mother had a belief in me which had nothing to do with logic, and this may have been connected with an extra-sensory gift she sometimes displayed. I remember one day during a school holiday, driving to Ilfracombe with her in order to visit an old lady who had, at one time, been a nurse to my father. The idea of the visit was really an excuse for a holiday diversion, because my mother had no knowledge of the old lady's address. I was, therefore, impressed by my mother when, soon after our arrival in Ilfracombe, as we were walking down a street, she suddenly stopped outside a house and said: 'I feel she lives here.' And the old lady did.

My mother did not want us to leave London because it meant the breaking of day-to-day contact; the end of an era. Jeannie's mother inevitably looked upon our departure in the same way, but neither my mother nor hers tried to make us change our minds. We were living, at the time, in the house with a roof like a dunce's cap opposite the finishing post at Mortlake. Here we had our Boat Race parties with guests from Jeannie's glamorous Savoy world; and it was here, on Boat Race days, that Monty, Ambrose's double, used to sit in the window, admired by the milling crowds outside, with a pale blue ribbon as a collar. We let the house when we first came to Cornwall (we had an unfurnished tenancy), but a couple of months later we were startled to learn that our tenants had disappeared overnight. My mother took charge of the situation. Every day she travelled to Mortlake from her home in Chelsea, proceeded to do any housework that was needed, and to undertake the tiresome task of showing round new prospective tenants sent to her by the estate agents. Eventually, we gave up hoping for a suitable tenant, and we surrendered our own tenancy, sold much of the furniture, and the rest travelled to Minack.

My mother regularly visited us until she died. At first, she used to stay at the Lamorna Inn and I used to drive in our Land Rover to pick her up in the morning; and if it were during the potato season, she used to make herself useful by holding open the tops of the potato bags so that it was easier to pour in the potatoes from the baskets. Then, after we had bought a chicken house for £50 and had turned it into a spare room, she used to stay there. She loved Jeannie and, soon after the end of the Hitler war, she decided she would like to present Jeannie at Court. She herself had been presented when she was young, in the days when debutantes were dressed in flowing white dresses, queued in their carriages along the Mall, were ushered into the royal presence, and made curtsies which had been practised for weeks beforehand.

Jeannie's presentation did not have such an old-fashioned panache. She was one of several hundred at a Garden Party, and the royals were only seen at a distance, but she has always remembered the occasion with pride. My mother also enjoyed herself. A foible of hers was a worship of aristocracy, English, French, German, and she would sometimes talk of her Walter Mitty-like dream that elevated my father into the Earl of Glendorgal, my eldest brother into Viscount Porth (so named after our local village), and my other brother and myself into Lords. Fortunately, there was no chance of such a dream turning into reality, but the occasion of Jeannie's presentation gave her a chance to mix with the aristocracy she so admired, and she was not going to miss it.

Ten minutes after we had passed through Buckingham Palace into the gardens, she disappeared. Obviously, in such a large crowd it was going to be difficult to find her, but Jeannie and I pounded round and round, up to one end of the gardens, back to the other, hopefully believing that she, in her turn, was looking for us. She was not. The Garden Party had passed its peak, guests had begun to leave, when we suddenly saw her walking towards us.

'Monkey!' we called out in delight (my mother had this

curious nickname of Monkey), 'where *have* you been?'

She smiled happily. She had had the time of her life. She had found a tea tent full of aristocrats.

When she died, we invested her legacy in bulbs, seven tons of them. We bought a variety called Joseph McLeod from a bulb grower near Truro, and the remainder we bought from a silver-tongued Dutchman, who mesmerised us with the fluency of his sales talk. At this particular period, Dutch salesmen of bulbs were a vogue in West Cornwall. Their broken accents charmed the wives of farmers, and the farmers were charmed by the prospect of the daffodil profits which seemingly awaited them; and so, bemused by the words of the silver-tongued Dutchmen, many of them invested in bulbs. Unhappily for them, they had given little thought as to how the daffodils from the bulbs had to be marketed, giving no thought to the fact that daffodils, unlike turnips, are delicate things. No consideration, for instance, was given to the condition of the daffodils. Storm-damaged blooms, slug-ridden blooms, warped blooms, all were bunched, then jammed into a cardboard box which often itself was a damaged one, and despatched to one of the many markets of Britain. The result, in due course, resulted in fewer silver-tongued Dutchmen roaming the lanes of West Cornwall. Traditional farming was more dependable than daffodils.

Our own silver-tongued Dutchman was a middle-aged gentleman, with a bald head like Yul Brynner, called Zandbergen. There were other silver-tongued Dutchmen who called upon us, but it was Zandbergen who was our Daffodil Svengali. He was one of the great names in the daffodil world; a daffodil show judge in many European countries, and possessing an encyclopaedic knowledge of the history of each daffodil variety.

He it was who told us the origin of the Joseph McLeod daffodil, which we had bought from the bulb grower near Truro. A friend of his bred it in a nursery not far from

Rotterdam in the beginning of the Hitler war, and so precious was the seedling bulb that his friend kept it in a pot on the mantelpiece of his sitting room. The sitting room faced the main street of the village and, along it, German soldiers used to patrol, often making a sudden raid on a house to catch the occupants listening to the war news from the BBC in London. One night, as he and his wife were about to listen to his secret radio, he heard the footsteps of the soldiers coming to his front door. There was a pause. He waited. Then the sound of the footsteps retreated and faded away up the street. A minute later, he turned on the radio and over the air came a voice announcing the victory of El Alamein. Then, as was the habit in those days, the announcer ended the news by giving his name. Joseph McLeod was the name.

'To celebrate this great victory,' said the man excitedly to his wife, 'we will call our seedling Joseph McLeod!'

Joseph McLeod is a beautiful golden daffodil, a long-lasting daffodil once picked and, from our point of view, it has the advantage of being harvested over a period of time. We start to pick early in the season, and there may still be blooms to pick a month later, unlike other daffodils, which bloom in a rush, then finish. But Joseph McLeod is unfashionable. Do not ask me why. The same mysterious impulses operate in regard to daffodils as they do concerning dress shops, restaurants, pop stars, picture galleries and workshop theatres. One moment they are 'in', the next nobody wants to know them. The special rival of Joseph McLeod is a daffodil called Golden Harvest and, as far as the flower markets are concerned, its place as the most fashionable daffodil is at the moment unassailable. It always fetches a higher price than Joseph McLeod.

I remember the first time Zandbergen came to the cottage he stayed for hours, while Jeannie and I listened like two students in school. Daffodils, up to that moment, had just been daffodils, and we had no knowledge of their history or of the vast industry that surrounded them. Daffodils had always been for me the sign of nature re-awakening; and when in London I bought my first bunch, I romantically believed they had come from some far meadow close to the sea. Zandbergen was to enlighten me that this was not so.

As long ago as the beginning of the century, daffodils were being forced in heated greenhouses, and by the thirties several million daffodils were being commercially forced in Lincolnshire. By the middle of the sixties, sixty million forced daffodils were coming onto the market, and by now the figure is probably nearer one hundred million and, because of new forcing methods like pre-cooling, they begin to be available in the shops from November onwards. Clearly this may be a practical advantage, but it seems sad that they have lost their role as the heralds of Spring, and become an industry like that of battery hens. Nevertheless, there are still the Scilly Isles and Cornish natural-grown daffodils available, but you have to ask for them specially and, except for the sweet-scented Sol d'Or from the Scillies, you will not see them in the shops before January.

Zandbergen, on that first visit, also solved a puzzle which had for long confused me. What is a narcissus? How does it differ from a daffodil? I ought to have known, I realise that, but there are some questions that one allows to lie in abeyance for such a length of time that it becomes an embarrassment to ask them. I have experienced the same embarrassment regarding the naming of a person whom I have met regularly, but whose name I did not catch at the moment of the first introduction. I have not dared to show my ignorance, and I have, therefore, greeted my new, unnamed friend with exaggerated phrases of *bonhomie* like: 'How *are* you, my friend?' Or: 'Dear fellow, what will you have?' For a period one can carry on in this way a friendly relationship without knowing the name of your friend but then, inevitably, comes the moment of crisis. Sometimes the crisis is caused by the need to introduce the new, unnamed friend to an old friend. Faced with this situation once, I tried to brazen it out.

'I have always wanted to ask you something,' I said to my unnamed friend, '*how* do you spell your name?'

He looked at me, surprised.

'I never thought Gibson was difficult to spell,' he replied.

The daffodil – narcissi puzzle also had a simple solution. Daffodils came into fashion towards the end of the last century when tenants of the Duchy of Cornwall in the Isles of Scilly began despatching them to Covent Garden. There was much debate at that time as to what they should be called, since Narcissus was the botanical name for all the varieties. However, in order to separate the trumpet varieties from the poeticus varieties, it was decided that the trumpets should be called daffodils, and the poeticus called narcissi. This is no longer the case; the whole of the narcissi family are now called daffodils.

Descendants of Zandbergen's daffodils still populate Minack in the spring. We bought from him the bulbs of the California, of the Dutch Master, of Early Bride, Brunswick, and Barrett Browning. Only his Golden Harvest have failed, the fashionable Golden Harvest, and the reason being that they did not like our soil and they developed basal rot and gradually died out. Other bulbs, bought at the same time ... the Joseph McLeod, the Hollywood, the Actaea ... all these also have their descendants populating Minack, and some of these were in the galvanised tins waiting to be bunched as I teased Jeannie for her remark 'how impermanent is permanence'.

I suppose it was unfair of me to tease her. Her remark was only reflecting a sudden mood of nostalgia, and I could imagine what she was remembering. Geoffrey, who once worked for us, lugging the daffodil baskets up from the cliff, then lifting them up on the bench and distributing the contents among the tins. Jane, the fourteen-year-old, with long fair hair, who came barefooted across the fields one day and informed us that she was going to work for us, that she was not going to school because she preferred flowers to lessons. Fran, the Australian girl on a world tour, who stayed with us for a flower season. Shelagh, the gentle, illegitimate girl, who deftly used to bunch the posies during the time we grew wallflowers, violets and calendulas, and who was to die a week after her twenty-first birthday. Boris, the Muscovy drake, who was brought to us by Jane. Monty, Lama, Oliver ... there was cause for her nostalgia as she bunched in the same small greenhouse they all knew so well. Even Penny, the donkey we bought one evening from the Plume of Feathers pub near Redruth, used sometimes to visit us as we bunched.

'I've done enough for the moment,' said Jeannie.

She was picking up the bunches which lay flat on the bench, counting them as she did so, putting twenty-five in a tin so that, when she came to pack them, fifty in each flower box, it would be quick to do.

'I'm going to look for Ambrose,' she said, as she went out through the door, 'Why not come with me?'

THREE

Ambrose was called Ambrose because Jeannie shone a torch on him when he was a kitten, and thought his soft ginger fur, in the torchlight, had the colour of amber. Her illogical reasoning then made her think of the musk rose in the garden in front of the bedroom window. Amber ... Rose ... and so, by this process of thought, Ambrose became Ambrose.

There is also a St Ambrose. We heard about him a little while after our Ambrose had been given his name. The saint was a distinguished lawyer who lived in Italy during the fourth century and became a Roman Catholic priest and a famous preacher. He had a special love for animals, and he used to preach in his sermons that the Roman Catholic dogma of animals having no souls and that man alone is a spiritual being was wrong. The dogma resulted, he declared, in great cruelty being inflicted on the animal world and he pleaded that the dogma should be ignored and that animals should be treated with kindness. Strangely, at the time that

Ambrose came into our lives, the sermons were re-published in Italy.

We went together into the Orlyt, which is the name of the first greenhouse we ever had, a hundred feet long and twenty feet wide. It stretches down to the stream in front of the cottage and, at the cottage end, Ambrose was curled on a green bolster which had been left there long ago by mistake, and where he and Oliver used to curl close to each other. We called it their day-bed.

Ambrose looked at us from the green bolster, staring balefully.

'Stay with him,' said Jeannie, 'while I fetch some fish.'

Had it been Oliver, or Lama, or Monty, I would have walked over to him, bent down, picked him up, hugged him, but I could not do such things with Ambrose. Ambrose still had his inhibitions; still had echoes of those inhibitions which, as a kitten, made him run away as soon as he saw us. He would have run away now had I approached him, as if he were running away from a stranger. I had learnt to tolerate this behaviour because, at times, I was countered by great bursts of affection, of roaring purrs, and of the kneading of my knees as he lay on my lap in my corner of the sofa. It was just that he had some inborn distrust of the human race which he found great difficulty in dispelling.

Jeannie, in the beginning, was concerned by his behaviour, by the way he ignored the tempting saucers of milk, fish and chicken she put down for him, until she had disappeared out of sight. For Jeannie was unaccustomed to being ignored by cats. Unlike myself, cats had been part of her world from a child, and she belonged to the band of cat lovers who believe they only have to make coo noises, noises of exaggerated endearment, noises which merit certificates of insanity, for the cat in question to come running to them.

I, on the other hand, have never approved of such cat loving blandishments, and this is due to my anti-cat education. Cats were considered vermin in my family; cats were shooed away if they were seen near the house. Moreover, anyone who even voiced approval of cats was considered lower in the social scale than ourselves. Owners of alsatians, labradors and mongrel terriers ... nothing wrong with such people, but cat lovers!

I have, of course, now seen the light. For instance, while once upon a time I averted my eyes from the sight of a cat, I now *notice* cats sitting on walls as I drive along in a car, and *worry* about cats I see at the side of a road, poised to pounce on a movement in the hedge. Cats have become part of my world. I will admire a neighbour's cat. I will concern myself about a cat which lives around our Penzance car park. I will praise the wisdom of a cat who chooses to live in the tailor's shop I sometimes visit. I have fussed over the Penzance station cat, who seemed oblivious of the throbbing noises of the diesel engines.

And further to illustrate the change in my cat attitude since that day when Monty came into my life in Jeannie's office at the Savoy, when I asserted I would throw him over Hammersmith Bridge, there is my encounter with the cat I met in St Ives, where I had gone to visit the dentist. I was on my way to the surgery when I saw a large, fluffy ginger cat, dozing on a garden wall in one of those narrow streets. I approached him in a friendly fashion and put out a hand to stroke him. He shot out a paw, scratched me, and drew blood.

Once upon a time I would have shouted at him. This time, I pretended he had not hurt me and went on my way.

Thus I have changed in my attitude to cats, though there is an aspect of the cat world of which I will never be a part. I will never make the coo noises, the noises of exaggerated endearment in which cat lovers, besotted cat lovers, so often indulge. I intend always to remain aloof. I will always be as independent as a cat.

I do not, however, believe that my attitude has influenced cats against me. If a cat wishes to pay court to a human being, he will do so - coo noises or no coo noises. There was the occasion, for instance, at the height of my anti-cat days, when I paid my first visit to Jeannie's parents, who lived in a handsome house in Avenue Road, St Albans. Naturally, I was wanting to give a good impression of myself and, when I arrived, I was taken into the drawing room by her parents where tea was laid, and offered a seat by the window. Beside the seat was a small table and, upon it, I shortly placed the cup of tea which had been handed to me. Conversation was conventional and I was being at my most polite, when suddenly there jumped onto my lap a large, long-haired blue Persian. I lost my head; my good manners disappeared. Instinctively I threw it off my lap and over went the small table and my untouched cup of tea. The Persian was Tim, Jeannie's most loved cat.

'I wonder,' said Jeannie's mother after I had departed, 'whether marriage to such an anti-cat man is right for you, Jean.'

Years later, I was again to be favoured by a cat jumping onto my lap uninvited but, this time, I considered the act an honour, though an honour which I did not feel I deserved.

For a year, Oliver and Ambrose had been treating the cottage as their home or, more accurately, Oliver treated it as his home, while Ambrose treated it as an hotel. Oliver wallowed in the comfort of the sofa, in the pleasure of curling in a ball in front of the fire, in the luxury of a bed to sleep on and, above all, in the knowledge that whenever he appeared a fuss was sure to be made of him. Oliver could rely on us for love, and we could rely on Oliver. Not so Ambrose.

Ambrose, if the window were open, would appear in the sitting room, prowl around, demand milk and whatever was on the cat menu, gobble it, then away again. He maddened me by his behaviour, and especially he maddened Jeannie. He was uncatchable, like Tinkerbell. She would bend down as he was drinking his milk, believing that he had not noticed her approach and, just as she had her hands ready for the clasp, he would dart away. He had no wish to be loved, or to love. It seemed that he wanted to remain as wild as when I first saw him. Then, one evening, came the moment when I received the honour which I did not deserve.

Jeannie was sitting in a chair absorbed in a book, and I was in my usual corner of the sofa, reading A. L. Rowse's *Tudor Cornwall*, marvelling at his scholarship and the detail of his research ... when I felt my leg softly touched. I looked down expecting to see Oliver, but it was Ambrose. I froze. I had been ignoring him, telling Jeannie that I was fed up with his behaviour and saying that he had all the worst characteristics that anti-cat people believed of cats: selfish; greedy; unlovable; arrogant. All these things I had been driven to say about Ambrose ... and now he was at my feet, looking up at me, touching me with a paw. A second later, he had jumped onto my lap.

'Jeannie,' I whispered, 'don't react too sharply.'

She was still absorbed in her book.

'Jeannie,' I whispered again, urgently, 'just see what has happened ...'

She looked round.

'Derek!' she said.

I do not say she was envious, because it is not in her nature to be envious, but she certainly would have relished changing places with me. I would have done so. After all, while I had been continuously insulting Ambrose, Jeannie had been cossetting him, defending him, feeding him and making those coo noises to him of which I so disapproved. I admit I was emotionally touched by Ambrose's gesture towards me, but I knew it was undeserved. It should have been Jeannie's moment of triumph ... this moment when Ambrose first sat on a lap.

Jeannie had now returned to the Orlyt with a saucer of boiled coley. Coley always had a bewitching effect on Ambrose. Unlike human beings, cats consider coley a gourmet fish. Human beings, myself included, think it tasteless, but for cats, and for Ambrose in particular, coley is nectar.

'Here … Ambrose,' she said, putting the saucer down on the ground, '… coley.'

A minor advantage of living where we do is that we can observe the fishing fleet come and go, and so be aware when it is a good time to stock up with fish. We then go to Newlyn to see Roger Veal. His father Jimmy ran the business when first we had a freezer and stocked up with fish and, during this period, Roger was training to be a potter. Today, he is one of the best known potters in Cornwall but, his father having retired from the business, Roger spends more time filleting fish than he does on his pottery.

Although it is mainly a wholesale fish business, he also caters for individual customers. The premises, however, do not resemble those of a conventional fishmonger. The building faces Newlyn river, five minutes from the fish market and, after climbing a dozen steep steps, you find the available fish heaped in wooden boxes … plaice, pollack, mackerel, ling, turbot, coley, John Dory. John Dory, an ugly looking fish with a subtle flavour, used to be Ambrose's favourite, the favourite of Lama and Oliver also, until it became so expensive that it became a luxury both for the cats and ourselves. So it is coley we order for Ambrose; 20p a lb when he was a kitten; now around 70p a lb, and we buy it by the stone, ready filleted by Roger. We take it home, put the fillets in polythene bags, three or four fillets in each bag, and feel relieved that Ambrose's larder is full for the next few weeks. Coley, of course, is not his only diet. But it is coley which he usually finds irresistible.

Not on this occasion.

'Come on, Ambrose,' said Jeannie, trying to lure him in a soft voice, 'it's coley … you know how you love coley.'

Ambrose did not budge from the bolster.

'He's off his food,' I said. 'It's understandable.'

'He didn't eat anything yesterday and, during the night, I

32

heard him miaowing outside the bedroom window.'

'I did too ... don't forget this is the first time he had been on his own. It will take time for him to get used to.'

The Orlyt, at this particular period, was not a pretty sight. A fortnight previously, a gale, a hurricane of a gale, had swept across Cornwall, ripping off roofs, blowing down electricity power lines and damaging greenhouses. The Orlyt had been one of the greenhouses. The sight of it, as Ambrose lay on the bolster, made me think of a heavily bandaged, wounded soldier. The glass on the sea side was in smithereens and the wooden frames broken and, for temporary repairs, we had draped yards of polythene along the side, hopefully kept in place by a combination of wood lathes and staples. It was a hotchpotch job, but safe enough, we hoped, until proper repairs could be made.

Ambrose continued to stay on the bolster, continued to stare balefully.

'Oh well,' said Jeannie, 'I'll leave the plate here for you and you can have it when you're ready for it.'

She was not being impatient. She was being practical. Ambrose did not want us to hang around, cossetting him, imposing our sympathy upon him. As it is often with human beings, he wanted to come to terms with his new situation by being alone.

'Let's go back to our bunching,' I said.

We too were sharing sadness. I hid it by making a flippant joke or two; Jeannie by silence. We had loved Oliver, vulnerable Oliver, funny old Oliver with his tail as thin as a twig, his link with Lama, and his astonishing gift to us of Ambrose. Some people cringe from displaying love for an animal and, when they see others displaying it, they accuse them of being sentimental as if sentimental were an insulting word. Such people seem scared of love. Perhaps it is because love is ephemeral; no rational reasoning about it because its base is emotion, unpredictable emotion, and this upsets some people because they are unable to define it in logical terms. Their world, in which they feel at ease, lies on intrigue and political manoeuvring and mocking at proven values. Mention love and they feel embarrassed.

We left the Orlyt and returned to our flower bunching. Then, after lunch, I took twenty boxes to Penzance station to catch the flower train to Paddington and Covent Garden. Penzance station acts as a market barometer for me. The big growers are continually on the telephone, ringing around the markets and finding out prices but, since we have no telephone, I rely for the most part on the news I glean when I am at the station. A porter will tell me, for instance, that a certain big grower is stockpiling his daffodils in his cold store pending an improvement in market prices. Or, as on this occasion, a grower will groan with me that the spring was far too mild and that, as a result, the price we received scarcely paid our expenses. For, apart from the general cost of looking after the daffodils, of picking, bunching and packing them, we have to pay both for the flower boxes and for the rail charges.

Jeannie was waiting for me when I returned home, the donkey halters in her hands . . . and news of Ambrose. She had found his coley plate empty and he was back on the bolster, curled up asleep.

'That's a relief,' I said.

'Now it is the donkeys we have to look after,' she said.

I laughed.

'What's happened?'

'Fred has been hooting his head off,' she said. 'They want a walk. They haven't had a walk for a week.'

'Have we time?'

'I think we can spare them an hour.'

Daffodil time was always a bad time for the donkeys. Their grazing was restricted because land where they would have grazed during other parts of the year, was now the home of the daffodils. Hence, for the most part, they were restricted to the field above the cottage, and this gave them a chance to stand at the edge of the field by the cottage and look down at us and hoot.

I should not have used the plural. Fred would hoot, but Merlin, prize-winning Merlin; Merlin, whose breeder forecast when he was a foal was that he had a great future in the prize-winning ring; Merlin, who is in the Donkey Breed Society stud book, could not hoot. He had been with us four years and not a hoot.

Merlin had come to us after Penny, Fred's mother, had died. Fred, disconsolate, had been on his own for nearly a year when we saw in the Donkey Breed Society bulletin an advertisement extolling the virtues of an eighteen-month-old donkey whose home was at Skinner's Bottom, near Redruth. The language of the advertisement attracted us in any case, but we were also influenced, Jeannie in particular was influenced, by the fact that Skinner's Bottom was only a mile away from where we had bought Penny, Fred's mother. We had gone one evening for a drink at the Plume of Feathers at Scorrier. Next morning, I found I had bought a donkey.

Merlin was funny to look at; Fred was sedate. Merlin had a long, chocolate brown coat, stocky legs which appeared as though he were wearing old-fashioned plus-fours, and there was a fringe over his eyes like the fringe which covers the eyes of an Old English sheepdog. Fred's coat was a light brown and short. Fred was not in the stud book. Penny, we were told when we bought her, came from Connemara and had been shipped along with a concourse of donkeys to Britain via Fishguard, and thence she was transported by a dealer to Exeter, where she was sold at an auction and taken to Cornwall. First to a field just outside Camelford, then to Scorrier, then to Minack. Soon after we bought her, we traced the dealer concerned, and he told us that he had no intention of buying a donkey when he went to the market. When Penny came up for auction, however, he thought her so beautiful that he could not resist bidding for her. Penny was a black donkey and, at the time, she was in foal to Fred.

'Where shall we take them?' I asked.

'Perhaps to Carn Barges and the far feeding grounds.'

This was a regular walk and we called it the donkey walk. It was a walk along the coastal path until we reached Carn Barges, then we turned inland along a path which led us eventually to what we called the far feeding grounds, meadows of rough grass above Lamorna Cove. The donkeys had a special liking for this rough grass. Carn Barges, Cornish for kite rock, is a huge rock standing as if on a pedestal and with a cascade of multi-shaped rocks falling steeply to the sea below it. It was from here that we first saw Minack those years ago; Jeannie on holiday from the Savoy Hotel, myself from MI5.

The path inland from Carn Barges has always been a rough one, brambles and bracken crowding in from the sides, and it always has been a special charm of this path that it is so wild. It was not an official path and it was left to us and to other locals to keep it open. It was, in fact, a path specially for the few who enjoyed its loneliness and did not mind sometimes having to push themselves through the undergrowth.

The admirable coastal path, on the other hand, caters more for the many. Hikers pound along it, vast packs on their backs, heads down, seemingly oblivious of the scenery.

'A beautiful walk!' said Jeannie to one group of such hikers.

'Is it?' came the reply, heads facing the ground. 'Haven't had time to look.'

The path to the left winds its rough way towards a small wood and a stream. It is a narrow, fast-running stream which tumbles down to the sea, zig-zagging its way through the boulder-strewn cliff land. Fred was frightened of the stream when first he saw it. He would look at it, then back away and, while Penny had waded through it without fuss, Fred would remain with hooves anchored to the ground, refusing to budge. He gained confidence, in due course, and there was one occasion when, instead of wading, he crossed it with a magnificent leap.

By chance, the day of this achievement was both Jeannie's birthday and the day of the Grand National, and among the runners of the National was a horse called Fearless Fred. Fred's magnificent leap, therefore, seemed to be of some significance and so, on returning to the cottage after the walk, I made some excuse to Jeannie that I had to go into Penzance. I hastened to a betting office, put £5 on Fearless Fred for a place and, on my return, placed the betting slip in a large envelope, made a hole in one corner of the envelope through which I threaded a long string and, in large letters, wrote on the envelope: Happy Birthday! I then went and found Fred and I tied the envelope around his neck, then led him to the cottage door, calling out to Jeannie to open it. Her pleasure was such that she gave Fred a large piece of her birthday cake. That afternoon, her pleasure was even greater. Fearless Fred had come third in the National at twenty to one, and so Fred's magnificent leap across the stream by the wood had won her £20.

Merlin also, when first facing the stream, dug his hooves in and refused to budge. We tried to persuade him to move in the manner of racecourse attendants who push reluctant racehorses into their stalls at the beginning of races. Fred, on the other side of the stream, nonchalantly grazed while I was pushing Merlin's bottom and Jeannie was pulling on his halter. When at last we persuaded him to cross the stream, Jeannie fell into it as she tugged at the halter ... but then

Merlin was over, and we had no trouble with him again.

Merlin, this spring, caused us another problem, though of a different nature. This time he was not digging his hooves in, being obstinate. This time it was greed which caused the problem.

Jeannie and I and Margaret, our potter friend who lives at the end of the lane, were picking the Joseph McLeod daffodils in the Lama field close to the cottage and above the bridge. The donkeys were in the big field we call the donkey field, and it is so placed that it is easy to see them from where we are picking. There came a moment when, after a period of bending down, picking the daffodil stems, I stopped and stood up, stretching myself.

I was standing there when I saw Merlin pushing forward his neck across the far hedge of the donkey field, and a figure on the other side of the hedge was offering him something white. I should have gone and investigated but I was tired and caught in the picking routine and, after a pause to stand up, I continued with my picking. My lack of curiosity nearly cost Merlin his life.

Early in the afternoon I made my trip to Penzance station with the daffodil boxes. On my return, I decided it was time for me to rotovate one of the greenhouses where, in a fortnight's time, we would be planting the tomatoes. We used to grow around three thousand tomato plants, and we used to heat the greenhouses with hot air blowing through polythene tunnels. But labour costs, and the cost of oil, have made such a programme impossible, and so we now grow five hundred plants in a greenhouse without heat and which we look after ourselves. It was to this greenhouse that I drove the small rotovator.

A blackbird sat on the glass roof and watched me as I arrived. He was no doubt anticipating the pleasures to come. Blackbirds have a great interest in our tomato growing, maddening us in the process. They impatiently wait as the plants grow, as the yellow flowers turn into green pebbles and swell and turn yellow; and when the tomatoes start to turn red, they swoop.

They swoop through the vents which I have opened on a summer day, and hop along the rows, plunging a beak into this tomato or that. We curb anger by pretending we are paying for a blackbird's song. A noble outlook, maybe, though reality challenges our patience. Lovely round tomatoes with great gouges in them hanging on the plants; other gouged tomatoes lying on the ground. We leave them where they are, hoping the blackbirds will continue to peck at them instead of pecking at fresh ones.

I completed my rotovating, had tea, and decided it was time to bring the donkeys down from the field above the cottage to the stables, which was really just an old barn, and where an armful of hay awaited them. This was their night quarters, although the way was open for them to go to the adjoining field if they so wished. When I called to them, Merlin was slow in coming and this surprised me because it was usually Fred who held back. Fred seemed to enjoy keeping me waiting. It was a means of proving his independence, and sometimes this made me cross. The halter in my hand, anxious to get the transfer over as quickly as possible, I would have to stand by the gate calling Fred until, at last, he'd deign to arrive.

It was a Monday, and on Mondays I load our dustbin in the back of the Volvo and drive up to the top of the lane, where I deposit the dustbin, which is collected early on Tuesday morning by the Council's refuse lorry. As I got into the car, bearing in mind Merlin's slow way of walking, I called out to Jeannie to have a look at him.

'He seems to be very lethargic,' I said.

I went up the lane, dumped the dustbin in its usual place, turned the car and drove back. It is a narrow lane with a ditch alongside much of its length. In summer, when each side is dense with such wild flowers as old maid's lace and clumps of pink campion, it is even narrower. Although, in due course, I cut these sides down, I postpone the task for as long as possible. One reason is that the lane is so beautiful in its wild state, and another is that it provides fledglings a place in which to hide during those first few days after leaving the nest.

Nonetheless, the lane causes problems for some drivers. An American couple from San Francisco once appeared, apologetically, at the cottage door with the news that their car was wedged in the ditch. And another time, a young man arrived to tell us that his van was at right angles in the ditch near Monty's Leap, that he had driven from London and that his mother was inside it with their four cats which they had brought to show us. Then he added that his mother was a cripple and could not get out. Both situations were dealt with successfully. The Americans showered us with chocolates, and the son and his mother have kept in touch with us ever since.

I was greeted by an anxious Jeannie on my return.

'You're right,' she said. 'Merlin is ill. He's trying to be sick and you know what that means.'

Donkeys cannot be sick. Their internal mechanism does not allow them to be sick, and so the poison pours out of their nostrils, some of it, and the rest congeals in their insides and colic develops and, unless they are attended to sharply, they will become paralysed.

'All right, I'll go and ring the vet straightaway.'

We have never had a telephone at Minack. There is a conventional explanation for this. We do not like, for instance, the threatening ring of its bell. Too much gossip is channelled through a telephone. Too many remarks which are later regretted. There are also the people who ring you up who you do not want to talk to, who press you to accept invitations which you do not want to accept. If you have no telephone, people have to think twice about contacting you, so the first impulse to do so often withers and, therefore, you are spared. If the first impulse is truly sincere, a telegram will arrive, asking us to ring such and such a number, kindly adding that we should reverse the charges. Not having a telephone and the threat of its bell also helps to create a sense of timelessness; and a by-product of this advantage results in friends who come to lunch, stay for tea, stay for drinks, and all the while conversation is flowing without the interruption of a telephone ringing, which would remind us all that time is passing. There are also more practical reasons why we do not have a telephone. Both Jeannie and I, if the truth be told, are born telephone talkers. Jeannie had three telephones on her desk at the Savoy, while I was called by my family a telephone king. Hence, if we now had a telephone, a telephone where we had only to put a finger on a dial and reach any part of the world, we could soon be broke.

There are, however, the disadvantages. There will always be, from time to time, moments of crisis, and there was now this crisis concerning Merlin. As a result of having no

telephone, I had to race to the call-box at Sheffield, a hamlet with an incongruous name, which was three miles away on the road to Penzance.

I found our regular vet was off duty. The one on duty lived at Hayle and that meant he was nearly twenty minutes away. I have found before that vets are quicker to respond to an emergency than doctors. We once had a guest who had a sudden collapse and, as our admirable personal doctor was on holiday, my phone call was automatically put through to the relief. The relief's wife explained that he was out and, in any case, we lived out of his area. She advised me to call an ambulance. Before doing so, I rushed back to the cottage ... and, thankfully, found the guest recovering.

The vet from Hayle was with us, examining Merlin, within half an hour, and injected him against colic.

It was just as well that he had come to us so quickly.

'Another four hours,' said the vet, 'and I could not have done anything to save him.'

The well-wishing figure I had seen had given Merlin, the vet guessed, a meat sandwich. Meat is poison to a donkey.

FOUR

I envy placid people. I envy those who appear to lead normal lives, to have normal relationships, normal emotions. The complications of life which pursue the rest of us do not seem to affect them. They do not seem to suffer from imaginary fears or financial worries or contradictory secret thoughts. If you go into their homes, you find the rooms are tidy, the furnishings apparently new, fresh paint on the woodwork, and not a speck of dust to be seen. Their homes are as well organised as their minds. Everything is under control. There is never a reason for them to wake up in the early hours of the morning and worry.

I have always been a worrier. I have spent months of my life worrying in the early hours of the morning because I have never been able to take happiness for granted. Happiness, in my imagination, should be like a calm lake without a ripple upon it; and no prospect of a ripple. Unfortunately, although there have been many times that I have seen this calm lake, my imagination has also seen the ripples that might come.

An example happened today; a trivial example maybe, but the incident concerned awoke in my mind a worry that I have from time to time. I was checking the engine which pumps the water from our well. The well is fifty yards up the hill above the cottage and, close by, there is a low hedge, the other side of which is the donkey field. I had finished checking the engine and was idly watching the donkeys grazing, when I saw a large fox appear through the gap at the top left hand side of the field. It was half past twelve; a strange hour for a fox to be around.

It began to lope across the field towards the wood. It moved slowly, then rested, then moved on again. I saw Merlin watching it, and the way he was doing so amused me. Had it been a dog, Merlin would have been running at him, head down, intent on chasing him away, but this fox ... Merlin, a puzzled Merlin, seemed to be saying: 'What on earth are you doing around at this time of day?'

The worry that the sight of the fox awoke in me was twofold. First, in its slowness, I thought it might be sick which, in retrospect, I do not think was the case. Secondly, I was reminded of the current persecution of foxes which, in my view, is far more unpleasant than hunting. I refer to snares and gin traps, both of which are still used for catching foxes.

I am passive in my opinion about fox hunting, provided it is genuine fox hunting and not the monstrous hunting of a fox which has been domestically bred, then deliberately released in a fox-hunting country. Such acts, and they do happen, should be subject to criminal law. Genuine fox hunting can be excused as a sport which gives the fox a chance to escape and, in any case, the chief victims of fox hunting seem to be the occupants of the land over which the horses charge. I have seen a field of cabbage in ruins. But the snares and the traps! These are the things which the anti-cruelty bodies should concentrate upon.

There is an export market for fox pelts. There is a

European market and a Japanese market, and the price is around £30 a pelt. This means it is a lucrative business to catch foxes, provided the pelts are undamaged. It is no use peppering them with gunshot and, obviously, no use for a hound to savage a fox. Hence the traps and snares. They are agony; slow torture. Those who use these methods are often only doing it for beer money.

Thus I had a ripple of worry as the dog fox disappeared into the wood out of my sight, out of Merlin's sight; a worry caused by my imagination wondering how long it would be before this tired, old fox was also caught in a snare or a trap.

I am, from time to time, pestered by other unnecessary worries. I have worried often that I have talked too much at a party, and said things which I did not really mean. I worry, of course, about world conditions, but that particular worry is universal. I worry about the greenhouses and their condition. I worry, in moments of hypochondria, about myself. I worry about the memories of long-ago meetings, which remain so fresh in my mind that I can vision the occasions and, in retrospect, be aware that the cause of their failure was my fault. I worry about anything in my small world, if I am in the mood. I am one of those people, therefore, who are labelled insecure by those who beam self-confidence.

There was, however, a special worry for Jeannie and myself which concerned our environment. It was a worry which surfaced from time to time when we saw activity on the other side of the valley.

The other side of the valley belonged to Bill, a farmer friend of ours. The land, except for two fields, was moorland, though in winter when the bracken was beaten down one could see the outline of stone hedges that had been painstakingly built decades ago. Our farmer friend, when he first took over the farm, proceeded to open up this moorland and plant potatoes and, in some places, daffodils. After a while, he found, as we also found, that the risk of growing potatoes, the risk of a frost or of a gale, the risk of a glut when one was harvesting them, was not financially worth the effort involved. He gave up working the moorland himself. He let Mary his daughter and Mike her husband work the land in their spare time, for both had regular work.

They were a handsome couple; both dark, Mary slim and pretty, Mike with the rugged Cornish looks that the Newlyn School used to like to paint. Mary, when she was a schoolgirl and we kept Rhode Island Reds, a dozen of them in a patch of ground near the cottage, used to come and feed them and shut them up at night if we were away. Mike was always ready to help in any emergency. Once, when we were snowed up, the lane feet high in snow, he waded through the drifts just to see that we were all right. And the day when the two Americans from San Francisco turned their car on its side in the ditch, it was Mike who heaved it out. While they worked the moorland, or part of it, our environment was safe. But supposing they too decided the work involved was too much for them? That was the worry.

It is a worry that affects everyone who lives in a lovely place. There you are in your home surrounded by fields and, one day, you hear by chance that the land is being sold around you and sanction for a housing estate has been approved; or you learn that the by-pass around your local town is going to take a slice of your garden. You chose your home because you wanted to be away from the crowd. You were happy in your isolation, and then suddenly you have been swept back into the maelstrom from which you were so anxious to escape. Sadly, you find that people do not understand your horror. You are selfish, is the message, to wish to live isolated in countryside which can be used for the homeless. The message seems so logically correct. Why should the individual ever stop the many?

It was on a January day, before the daffodil season had begun, when Oliver was still alive, that I heard the groaning of a machine coming down the lane, then the appearance of a bulldozer in the large field on the other side of the valley.

'Jeannie,' I called out. 'Come and look ... what are they doing?'

We could see half the Oliver field from the cottage, the other half was obscured by the trees around Monty's Leap ... a two acre field on a slope and the gate which led into it was fifty yards up the lane on the right from the Leap. Thus the western hedge lined our lane, while the bottom hedge, at right angles to the lane, lined the undergrowth which surrounded our small reservoir whence came the water for the greenhouses. This bottom end, therefore, was virtually on our doorstep. Here our privacy was at its most vulnerable. Understandably, I was worried. Why had Bill, our friend and neighbour, called in a bulldozer?

The clanging, the heaving roar, the metallic noise of a bulldozer lunging at rocks, is one of the most disquieting I know. The angry-looking machine is so quick in its destruction. A thousand years of history is destroyed in half an hour ... woods, badger setts, fox's earths, ancient pastures, ancient hedges, ancient buildings obliterated between the time the driver arrives for work and his morning break for a cup of tea. Once upon a time, there was a time to think before ordering such destruction. Hand labour was no bulldozer. Hand labour, with its shovels and pick axes, gave the instigators of destruction time to change their minds. A brake, therefore, existed to prevent the destruction of the English countryside. A brake still exists, though in another form. The many conservation groups represent this brake. Their objections to change, their patient, often very expensive challenges against the rape of the countryside, act as the hand labour with its shovels of other days.

We watched our particular bulldozer from the bridge, that corner a few yards from the cottage where we look out across the moorland to the space of Mount's Bay and the long outline of the Lizard, and where it seems we are standing on the bridge of a ship.

'Silly,' I said, 'how easily we panic.'

'No wonder ... that bulldozer could tear through the moorland and change the whole landscape.'

'How I wish we could own that land and make it safe.'

'We own it in our minds. Every day of our lives we look out upon it. It belongs to us really ...'

'Dear, impractical Jeannie ... our minds don't hold the Deeds.'

'It is still part of our whole life.'

'You're in a fanciful mood, Jeannie. Let's be sensible. There's probably a simple explanation for the bulldozer.'

Indeed there was. The bulldozer had been brought in to remove the rocks which lay beneath the surface of many parts of the field, making the soil shallow, and so hindering the growth of good crops. A simple explanation ... yet why, I wondered, had Bill decided to rid the field of rocks when he had virtually retired from farming? It seemed curious.

In tranquil moments, the bridge is a wonderful place to be. I have spent many hours there just staring, thinking of nothing except to observe the movement of a fox, or the lazy flight of a buzzard; or watching the purposeful voyaging of a trawler towards Newlyn, or looking above me at the long plume of an air liner on its way across the Atlantic; or listening to the hum of bees among the pink flowers of the *escallonia* which borders the bridge, or wondering why the gulls were crying; or experiencing the sudden delight of remembering a moment when Monty, Lama, or Oliver had suddenly decided to join me on the bridge, rubbing against a leg.

Standing quietly on the bridge places living in perspective. The riches lie within oneself, if one has the discipline to discover them. Wordy speechs by do-gooders, generalising problems, generalising solutions, do not help one. The individual himself must make the effort to solve his own problems. The outsiders, those who offer blanket remedies, are conning us. It will always be the individual who will be able to create his own happiness. Ideas from others may help him find it. But no one, no politician, no do-gooder, no priest, can solve the tortuous, conflicting thoughts of the individual, except himself.

The daffodil season drifted to its end; not a successful one because the mild weather continued day after day. First we stopped picking the yellow daffodils then, after a two weeks' interval, there was the rush to pick the scented white Actaea; three days of picking and bunching and they also were finished. Actaea time is a painful one for Jeannie. Her eyes are allergic to Actaea. The dust of the pollen makes them smart, a form of flower rash, and she can never have a bunch of Actaea in the cottage. Flower rash affects many people during daffodil time, and what is so mysterious is that someone who has dealt with daffodils for much of their life will suddenly develop it. So far, I have been immune. So, too, has Jeannie, except for smarting eyes when the Actaea bloom.

The donkeys were pleased when the daffodil season was over. There was little pleasure being left in a field which they had nibbled over a thousand times. Fred would hoot for attention, and hootless Merlin would watch him, while Jeannie and I ignored them both. Thus, the daffodil season was a boring time for the donkeys, and when donkeys are bored they look for diversions.

One early morning, I had been picking daffodils in a meadow at the bottom of the cliff. I pick with the left hand, going up each bed of daffodils as fast as I can and, when my left hand can hold no more, I change the stems to my right hand. I continue thus until my right hand can also hold no more, and then I stop picking and carry the stems to the wicker flower basket, packing them upright and tight. At this stage, I will sometimes pause, take a rest, stare out to sea, or look along the coast towards the promontory of Carn Barges half a mile away, which is on the route of the coastal path. On this particular morning, I was having one of these rests when I suddenly saw the outline of two figures standing in the shadow of the rocks around Carn Barges. As it was only eight o'clock, very early for any walker to be about, I immediately became suspicious. They could be daffodil thieves.

We have to be wary of daffodil thieves, especially early in the season when prices are high. The coastal path, passing as it does through some of our meadows, enables people to pick our daffodils without hindrance, except for the typed notice I have on a board which reads: THESE DAFFODILS ARE COM-MERCIALLY GROWN. DO NOT PICK! Yet the occasional person will ignore such a notice. One year, I found a young man with a haversack full of our daffodils; another year, I caught a middle-aged couple picking through a meadow as if they were professional pickers, and this particular year, we had had a maddening experience.

One afternoon, a January afternoon when the season was about to begin, Jeannie and I had toured the meadows with the purpose of estimating whether there were enough daffodils to pick for our first box or two. When we looked at one special meadow, close to the coastal path, we decided there were enough daffodils in bud to fill at least a box, and so we decided to pick them on the morrow and send them away to market. The first box of the season. Always an exciting moment.

Early next morning, before we had our breakfast, we went happily to pick them.

They had gone. The juice of the picked stems was still wet. Somebody from the coastal path had reached the daffodils first.

Hence, when I saw these two figures in the shadow of the rocks on Carn Barges half a mile away, it was understandable that I was suspicious. I cursed that I had not brought my field glasses with me, but had left them at the top of the cliff, hanging on a bush. I should have continued to pick, keeping my curiosity under control, but I did not do so. I was still smouldering with anger over the disappearance of our first daffodils, and my undisciplined thoughts envisioned that up there on the Carn those two figures I could see in the shadow of the rocks might well be the culprits of that early morning daffodil theft.

I plodded up the cliff to the bush where I had left my field glasses.

I focused them on the Carn.

I saw no daffodil thieves.

Just two donkeys.

Two bored donkeys, who had escaped from their field by unlatching the gate in Houdini-like fashion.

Two happy donkeys, who had then galloped at speed along the coastal path to the Carn.

Two contented donkeys, munching the grass among the rocks.

I was a victim. A single person's theft had made me suspicious of everyone. Nothing very unusual. So often the behaviour of an individual can bias one against the integrity of the many.

The daffodil season was over, and we were able to relax and return to normality. There was, for instance, no hurry to rise in the morning, no looking at a watch and worrying about a train to catch, no pressures at an office, no sound of traffic, no telephone bell to ring. This was the peace which people dream about when their lives are pinioned in the stress of a city yet, along with this peace, comes a sense of guilt. Why should one be so lucky? How long will it last? And also there sometimes comes a sense of lassitude.

The lassitude I suffer from is an inability to make up my mind as to which of many tasks I should begin on. I will make a list of them, stare at the list, and do nothing. I will see on the list that a pane in one of the greenhouses has to be mended; the soil of the kitchen garden must be rotovated into a fine tilth for the seeds of the summer vegetables; I must cut down the stinging nettles under the apple tree; I must clean the ditch which borders the land and fill in the potholes with small stones; I must string up the tomato plants before the plants flop over; I must paint the cottage windows and the garden chairs and table; there are letters I have not answered, and my diary of the past fortnight must be filled. Each task on the list is numbered, and there are thirty of them. I just stare at the list. My lassitude has paralysed me into inaction.

Part of the fault lies in the fact that I was born in February under the sign of Pisces, which is that of two fish swimming in opposite directions. Pisces people, it seems, are indecisive, inclined too often to see two points of view which means they wobble when they have to make a choice. I do not think this is entirely fair. As a Pisces, I am aware that I can take a long time to make up my mind, am in favour of going over and over the facts of a problem, but there usually comes a time when I am inwardly sure of the decision that has to be made. The pursuit of inward sureness was also a consequence of my period in MI5, where I was closely associated with a man who was responsible for a very special area of investigation, and for whom I still have the greatest respect. He always advised me to discuss a case, and those involved in it, with a patience which should be endless, looking at it from every point of view, learning every detail of those concerned ... and then suddenly, he maintained, a chink would appear and the lead one was looking for would reveal itself. I have often maddened Jeannie by following this man's advice. 'Why,' she has often mocked me, 'can't you make up your mind?'

But this attitude of mine does not excuse my moments of lassitude. These are moments of sheer laziness; moments often induced by the weather, or the mindless sound of the Tater-du Lighthouse fog-horn which blares out not far away.

It is a remote control fog-horn so that if there is fog with a limiting three miles visibility at the Lizard lighthouse thirty miles away, or at the Coastguard Station at Porthgwarra five miles west down the coast, a button is pressed and Tater-du blares a twentieth-century metallic sound every thirty seconds. Too often the visibility is clear in the Tater-du area when the metallic sound blares. Too often there is not a ship to be seen. Too often the wind blows its noise inland and not out to sea. It is sadly ironic that one of Cornwall's greatest sea disasters, the wreck of the *Union Star* and the tragedy of the Mousehole lifeboat, should take place within a few hundred yards of Tater-du as the light flashed and the fog-horn blared.

Ambrose behaved that night, December 19th 1981, as he often behaves when a gale is blowing. We had called him to come in at dusk, but he was nowhere to be found. Gales fascinate him, or perhaps their noise as they tear through the trees and bushes provides admirable hunting conditions. He is, at any rate, obstinate when a gale is blowing; and he maddens me. I call and call and call, and he ignores me.

The gale was sweeping in from the south, and although I realised it was a bad one, the cottage was not receiving its full force because it was sheltered by the hill which slopes above it. The gales that always shatter us blow from the east or the south east, roaring unchecked across the expanse of Mount's Bay.

We had supper, and there was still no sign of Ambrose, although I had left the bedroom window ajar for him. Around a quarter to nine, I switched on the television with the idea of leaving it on until the nine o'clock news. Then Jeannie said there had been an alteration in the programme schedule, and that the news had been changed to ten past nine. I switched the television off.

I waited five minutes, then went to the bedroom, opened the window wide, shone my powerful torch down the lane, and began shouting again into the gale: 'Ambrose! Ambrose!'

I had been there a few moments when out of the shadow beside the barn scurried a shape; and a second later Ambrose jumped on the window ledge, and was receiving my words of welcome. As this happened I became aware of the sound of an engine out to sea. The sound was at one moment high pitched, then suddenly muffled; and it made me think of the revving engine of a motorcar when its wheels are skidding in snow. When I returned to the sitting room I remarked to Jeannie about it.

'A boat out there,' I said, 'is having a struggle to get back to Newlyn.'

I thought no more about it. We are accustomed to boats struggling in heavy seas. If they are in trouble, we see flares, or are alerted by the drone of a Rescue Helicopter; or, in extreme cases of danger, coastguards will drive down the winding lane, and spread out along the cliffs.

I saw no flares as I stood at the window, heard no drone of a helicopter ... and there was no sign of a coastguard.

In the early hours of the morning, Ambrose snugly asleep between us, I thought I saw a glaze of unusual light in the sky. But there was a moon that night, and I explained it away that what I had seen was the light of the moon suddenly appearing from behind a cloud.

But just before dawn I was awoken by the headlights of a car flooding the bedroom. Past experience made me aware that a car at such an hour meant a wreck; and I jumped out of bed, put on my dressing gown, and a jersey over it.

'Two cars. Three cars,' I heard Jeannie call. 'Five cars!'

On a clear, sunny day, three cars arriving down the lane means a traffic problem. But five cars in semi-darkness!

They were the TV crews, ITV and BBC; and I went down to

meet them, and they told me the tragic news of the wreck of the *Union Star* and the loss of the Mousehole lifeboat.

Bearded George Lawry was with them as a guide. He and his articulate, remarkable wife Daphne, have the role of being spokesmen for the fishing community; and later, having been to the site of the wreck he explained to me, as he sipped a cup of coffee with us in the porch, how he had urged the BBC reporter to make a special mention of the plight of the eight lifeboatmen's families.

'If only we could raise a few hundred pounds' he said to me, 'to give to each family.'

Nearly three million pounds were raised.

There were the inevitable post event questions as to what had caused the disaster. My own interest, however, lies in the role of the coastguards. Up till a month previously, control of the coast was in the hands of the highly efficient local coastguards; and they had their headquarters at Gwennap Head near Land's End, and called Tol Pedn. These men knew every nook and cranny of the coast, every mysterious mood of the sea, every dangerous reef.

But a month previously, control of this lonely stretch of Cornwall had been transferred to Falmouth Coastguards with their spectacular modern equipment. They did not know our area and, although the *Union Star* was drifting helplessly for three hours towards the neighbourhood of Tater-du, they delayed sending out coastguards along the cliffs.

Had the coastguards spread out along the cliffs in force, they might have been able to keep watch on the lifeboat by firing flares; or, as I did, listen to the sound of the engines . . . so keeping track of the lifeboat's progress.

The lifeboat's radio went silent at 9.30 p.m.; and an hour and a half went by before anyone realised she had foundered. Soon after midnight the wreckage began to come in at Lamorna Cove; and to come in, as Jeannie and I discovered later that morning, into our own cove.

*

Ambrose also benefited now that the daffodil season was over, or I think he did. He was lost without Oliver. We understood that. In the month after Oliver died, Ambrose would not stay still. He kept wandering in the neighbourhood of the cottage, down into the stable field, down the lane and across Monty's Leap, and left into the field where the greenhouses stand. Then into the wood among the sweet-scented Sunrise daffodils, past Boris the drake's old house, and into the wood meadow where the donkeys shelter in winter and the owls hoot and where, in summer, a green woodpecker has its hole and warblers call. Ambrose was safe as he wandered, looking for Oliver. No man-made contraption threatened him. He was being natural amongst nature.

Yet there was a threat.

One night, as I lay in bed, I heard a miaow outside the bedroom window.

Cats, looking for homes, I was once told by a whimsical, besotted cat lover, have their own estate agencies. Cats who are thrown out by those who do not understand the subtlety of cats; kittens who are given as presents at Christmas, but who become a nuisance by the New Year; cats who interfere with holidays and are left to fend for themselves . . . such cats, I was told, go to their local cat estate agency and so discover where a home vacancy has occurred. The miaow I heard was possibly the miaow of a cat who had been told of a Minack vacancy.

Ambrose was on the bed when I heard this gentle, persuasive miaow and, as I lay there, my hand on the soft fur of Ambrose, I was astonished that another cat was offering to make a home with us so soon. It was indecent. It was an echo of that hasty cry: 'The King is dead. Long live the King!' Yet, and I thought this a faithless reaction on the part of myself, I had a sympathy for this unseen miaow. First Lama, then Oliver, then Ambrose, had come to Minack uninvited. Now there was another cat. I also experienced hope. It would be miraculous if another cat came to Minack in the same mysterious way that the others had come.

Ambrose did not share my feelings.

Ambrose stirred, sat upright, paused a second, then leapt at the window and growled. A deep, rolling growl which reminded me of summer thunder. A fearsome sound because a growling cat is displaying a special anger. A hissing, spitting cat is like anyone of us who has a fit of sudden fury. A flare up and it is over. But a growling cat reflects a deeper emotion, for he has borrowed a sound which one normally associates with his competitor, the dog. A growling cat, therefore, has been deeply affronted.

Or it may have been, in this case, a reflection of fear; a subconscious fear that his role in the household was threatened. Human beings react in this way. Human beings, when intuitively aware that a rival has come on the scene at home or in the office, will fence themselves in with imaginary barbed-wire. Ambrose fenced himself in with this growl.

'Come back, Ambrose,' I said, gently.

The moon was shining, silhouetting him against the soft, silver light, and I could see his tail swishing to and fro. Then he was out and away. Not silently, but with a string of cat epithets. The noise of them faded down the lane and half an hour later he was back on the bed. He had achieved his object. He had proved that he was the king of Minack.

The period when the daffodil season has ended seems suspended in time. Birthdays are over and the year stretches ahead with that always-forever feeling that one had as a child. There is freshness everywhere. There is the thrill of the first chiff-chaff, a swallow has still to appear, one is waiting for the call of the first cuckoo, swifts still have their long journey to make. One has the naive sense of awareness that simplicity, despite modern technology, remains the corner-stone of living. The white flecks of the stitchwort peer from the hedges; celandines, closed when the sky is overcast, beam when the sun shines. The bridal white of the blackthorn lines the lane, and wild violets spatter the grass of a meadow. A blackbird tops a leafless elder shouting its joy; a buzzard sails high, pale paths of currents trace a still, blue sea, and a sudden breeze rustles the *escallonia*. Pools of yellow gorse shine among the winter-beaten bracken; black and white cattle are a frieze on the skyline; a lark sings out of sight above me; and a woodpecker is tapping. The scent of the buds of the *trichocarpa* is sweet; a dunnock is chirruping; there is an early bluebell among the patch of rich green grass …

'Let's go for a stroll,' I said to Jeannie, during the morning after Ambrose's victory, 'just a wander round the meadows.'

'I can't just yet. I've got to make the bread.'

'All right, I'll wait.'

I have written about Jeannie's recipe for home-made bread, wholemeal bread and, occasionally, despite the chorus in favour of her recipe which came originally from her Scottish mother, there have been bleats from those who have had failures. Quite angry letters sometimes, as if it were Jeannie's fault that the dough had not risen, or the bread itself was as hard as cement. Cookery writers, I presume, must often have complaints by those who have failed to follow their recipes correctly. I wonder how they answer them?

Jeannie's recipe for wholemeal bread, and, if anything goes wrong after reading this, just try again, is quite simple:

3 lbs of wholewheat flour makes four pounds of bread.

Tip 1½ lbs of flour in a bowl, plus a tablespoon of salt, and a tablespoon of brown sugar. Pour in about 1½ pints of warm water, stir until you have the consistency of porridge. Meanwhile, you have put three heaped teaspoonsful of dried yeast in a half-cup of tepid water.

When it is soft and creamy, tip it into the flour mixture, leave it for fifteen minutes until bubbles appear. Now tip in remaining 1½ lbs of flour and stir with a wooden spoon, then knead it, or use a machine, until it turns into a stiff dough.

Now cut the dough into four equal parts and put them in four warmed, greased tins. Prick with a fork. In three-quarters of an hour, if placed in a warm place, the dough will have risen above the top of the tin. Put the tins in a very hot, pre-heated oven for three-quarters of an hour.

Do all this and you will never have to worry about a baker's strike. But the pitfalls into which people fall are these: never put the dried yeast into hot water because hot water kills the yeast (dried yeast in a tin is ready whenever you want to make bread, while natural yeast deteriorates); and always remember to prick the dough deeply with a fork before putting it to rise.

I waited until Jeannie was ready.

'I'll have three-quarters of an hour,' she said, 'while the dough is rising, then I must get back to put it in the oven.'

'Let's go,' I said.

There was no special reason, as we left the cottage, to go up to the bridge. It would have been normal for us, in view of the proposed stroll around the meadows, to turn left down the path towards the lane and the barn, and then turn right towards the cliff. But instead, curiously, we went up past the *escallonia* to the bridge and paused there, looking across to the other side of the valley.

Suddenly I said:

'Jeannie, look! There's Bill with a group of people!'

'Bill in his best suit!' said Jeannie.

'They're probably only relations.'

We continued to watch for a few minutes the other side of the valley and the little group, which seemed to be investigating the outlines of the long-ago meadows.

Then we went on our way.

FIVE

When Bill and his wife Kath lived at the farmhouse, they used to have holidaymakers to stay and the same holiday-makers would come back year after year.

The welcome they received, the delicious meals, the peace of their surroundings provided them with holidays they would always remember. Girls who came to help Jeannie and me during the daffodil season also used to stay there.

The first girl was a fair-haired, twenty-one-year-old Australian called Fran, who arrived at the cottage one January in a battered two-seater car, telling us that she was on a working tour of Britain, and that she was wanting to pick daffodils and, if we had no room for her to stay, she would be happy living in her car. But Bill and Kath took her in and she stayed with them for the daffodil season, walking down the lane each morning with a hold-all slung on a stick over one shoulder, and proceeding to pick daffodils with an energy and enthusiasm which inspired us when we were tired.

She writes to us still. She returned to Adelaide to her job as a hairdresser; then, weary of indoor life, she took a job as a shed hand, travelling round sheep stations in Australia and New Zealand. 'I badly wanted to be a shearer,' she said in a letter 'and at my first attempt I did a whole lamb in twenty minutes, which wasn't bad. I'm getting faster and faster, and my best time is ten minutes. Such hot work!'

Once she sent us a case of Australian wine because, she said, she was momentarily in funds. And the other day a letter arrived from her, saying she was now back home in Adelaide. 'Yesterday,' she said, 'I planted five punnets of Blazer Blue

Ageratum … then during a spell from gardening I sat down and read a few pages from the *Sun on the Lintel*, and found that you too had just finished planting the same plants. I thought it a lovely coincidence.'

Another daffodil season a New Zealand girl called Gail stayed with Bill and Kath. Gail, too, was on a working tour of Britain, and when the previous summer she had been employed in the kitchens of a holiday hostel in Penzance, she visited us at Minack, and offered to return in the spring. She was a slim, attractive girl and, in between her time in Penzance and her return, she had a job in Liverpool, where she had fallen in love. It would have been better if she had stayed in Liverpool. She was a sweet, kind girl, but she carried the image of her boy friend in her mind as she went about her work, and she was inclined to start to pick a row of daffodils, then stop and stare, and moon. She did not have the earthy brusqueness of a Fran.

Then there was Carol and, of the three, Carol fitted in most easily with the ways of Bill and Kath. It must have been difficult, I realised at the time, coping sometimes with the moods of Fran and Gail, evening after evening after they had returned tired, hours to go before bedtime, closeted all together in the farmhouse sitting room. There was television to watch, of course, but the farmhouse was far away from other distractions … Penzance five miles away, and only a rare evening bus. It must have been a strain sometimes for Bill and Kath; not that they ever showed it. But Carol was an easier companion.

Carol came to call on us during a summer holiday, and I met her coming down the winding lane after she had walked the main road from Penzance. She was a secretary at Courtaulds at the time and, before that, she had worked for a year in New York as a secretary. She was tall and slim, a sun-freckled face, long dark hair and, although she hated the glasses she had to wear, they suited her. She was quiet, and this Bill and Kath liked. They were at ease with her.

She lived at Cossall near Nottingham with her mother and, soon after her summer call on us, she wrote saying she could arrange to have a fortnight's holiday during the daffodil season, and we wrote back saying she would be welcome. She soon became a quick buncher but, strangely, she never mastered the art of picking. Perhaps she was too tall. Anyhow (and she was to be with us during other daffodil seasons), she became invaluable as a buncher, reaching the high standard of ten dozen bunches an hour. We no longer see her at daffodil time now. We see her instead when Jeannie or I have written a book. Carol then finds time to type it for us.

There came a time when Bill and Kath gave up the farmhouse to Mary and Mike, and they moved to a bungalow they had built a few hundred yards away down the lane towards the main road. Bill had green fingers and the rough ground around the bungalow was soon a panoply of flowers. At the back was a kitchen garden and, because I once told him I was hopeless at growing swedes and that my broccoli only developed to button size, he used to leave a swede or a broccoli at the gateway to the bungalow. They would always be there on a Friday, because that was the day he knew Jeannie went to Penzance in the morning. They would be there also on other days if he saw us outbound from Minack, and we would find them on our return; a couple of swedes or a broccoli on the hedge by the gate, so placed that we could not miss them.

We made occasional contributions from our own garden in return ... a greenhouse lettuce, a handful of tomatoes, and sweet peas which we grew in a greenhouse. Yet our most useful counter to Bill's gifts of swedes and broccoli were, in Jeannie's mind at any rate, the bones she gave Bill's dogs, Trixie and Meg. There had been other of their dogs Jeannie had given bones to ... Bounce, a spaniel, Flossie, a black and white sheepdog type, Trin, a dachshund, and there was also Whisky with the one blind eye. Jeannie was always saying to me as I set off in the car to Penzance: 'Please will you drop off these bones for the dogs?' They were lamb bones for the most part and, in view of what was to happen, it is important to remember that we often had a lamb bone to dispose of.

They had cats, too, at the farmhouse, and one of them was called Muffin, whom Jeannie believes was the mother of Ambrose. Muffin was not pretty. She was an assortment of colours: brown, black, grey, white, with a slash of orange across her face. At the time that Oliver was courting her, however, she had left the home of Bill and Kath and had joined the cats of Walter, who worked the adjacent farm ... Walter used to have so many cats that I called him the Pied Piper of cats. Oliver adored Muffin and we would find them along the lane during that particular summer, Oliver on one side of it, Muffin on the other, and Oliver staring at her entranced. Early that autumn we saw her several times down our end of the lane, close to Monty's Leap, though she scurried away as soon as she saw us. But what was she doing there? On October 10th, I first saw Ambrose.

A few days after we had seen Bill on the other side of the valley with a group of people, I was on my way to Penzance when I met him outside the bungalow. I stopped the car and we gossiped. He told me he had seen a colourful bird, a kind he had never seen before ... the size of a thrush, pink and blue, black and white. I said it sounded like a jay and that I was surprised he had not seen one before, because I had several times seen one in Lamorna woods. Then I told him about our squirrel.

Some weeks before, I looked out of our bedroom window one morning and there was this squirrel, jauntily coming up the middle of the lane towards the cottage. I am not acquainted with squirrels, and this one looked to me like a miniature kangaroo as it advanced nearer and nearer. Of course, I called excitedly to Jeannie, and the squirrel heard my voice and ran away past the Orlyt greenhouse into the wood. We searched for it that day, but never saw it again. Or perhaps we did. A fortnight later, we took a walk along the coastal path to the Pentewan meadows, where once we grew potatoes, and as we passed the old quarry we saw high up on a ledge ... a squirrel. Bill said he had never seen a squirrel in the area, though he had heard someone say they had recently seen one on top of a telegraph pole on the road to St Buryan. A lost squirrel. I suppose it must have come from Lamorna woods.

I left Bill for Penzance and, when I returned, a fat broccoli was waiting for me outside the bungalow gate.

May had come in with a cold east wind, bashing the pink blossom of the Japanese cherry tree, which I planted when my mother died, so that it scattered like confetti on the gravel in front of the barn. Petals of tulips fell away from their centres, a stem of a newly-planted, ten-week stock snapped, the white of the blackthorn was bruised brown. I never enjoy May in the manner that I should, whether it is cold or warm. The earth's bounty puts me under pressure. Wherever I go, I see work to be done. Grass is growing so fast in the ditch that sides the lane leading up to the farm that it will soon, unless I cut it down, cover the ditch and a car may slide into it. Ground elder must be cleared from the rose garden, the weeds must be picked up from the path leading to the cottage. Beneath the apple trees in the orchard the infant hogweed, and by now elderly Alexander must be slashed, but I do not want to do so because bluebells are in flower around them and the first of the cuckoo-flowers are to be seen; and of course nettles everywhere await attention.

Then there are the positive things to do. The succession of Fortune lettuces in the Orlyt, sown in January, look magnificent, but I must discipline myself to prepare ground outside and sow the seed for summer cutting. The dwarf sweet peas which I sowed in the Orlyt beside the lettuces have never germinated; perhaps I soaked the soil too much beforehand and the seed rotted ... but the sweet peas must be sown again. There was trouble too in one of the two large greenhouses where, alongside the early potatoes, I had sown a row of Early Onward peas. The row now resembled a straight run of miniature bomb craters ... mice had dug up the seed. The early potatoes had been a success and, before the end of April, we had begun to relish them. But in the neighbouring greenhouse, another May task was demanding my attention. The tomato plants required stringing up ... the tedious task of cutting the strings, standing on a ladder, tying the string to the overhead wire, while below me Jeannie pushed the wire stake into the soil and tied the other end of the string through the eye of the stake.

This catalogue of wearisome woes may suggest that I am rebelling against performing these necessary tasks, and that I am in the mood of those who, however fortunate they may appear to others, are always seeking to complain. My catalogue of woes, however, only reflects a momentary depression on my part. They are trivial. The kind of woes that affect anyone in one way or another, whether they live in a city or in the countryside. They are the woes of routine; the tasks that have to be done every day of our lives.

Yet one must also face up to the moments of true depression; the moments of sadness, of personal inadequacy, of loneliness, of fear of the future, which sweep one into an undefinable despair. Such despair is so personal that outsiders have difficulty in understanding it, or realising its depth. Of course, there are the professionals who are waiting to give advice, but their chief role, their most useful role, can only be to listen. There are also drugs and alcohol to tempt a person into illusory relief, into believing that despair can be banished by superficial means. But the only way to free oneself from despair is, I am sure, by one's own efforts, and by remembering the old adage of counting one's blessings and comparing oneself with those so obviously in a worse situation. As far as I am concerned, I remember a quaint piece of advice given me by a Chinese doctor I met in Shanghai during my tour of the world. The advice made me laugh, and it still does.

'When you feel despair,' he said, 'stop being self-analytical, or you will sink deeper and deeper.'

Then, he added: 'If you feel despair ... sing. Sing any cheerful song you can think of!'

Jeannie knows, therefore, what is happening when I sing.

Donkeys suffer from depression, or appear to do so. I have seen Fred in the centre of a green field looking gloomy; seen him with his back to a hedge in the rain looking gloomy; seen him even in the warmth of the stable on a winter's afternoon looking gloomy. 'Cheer up, Fred,' I have often said to him, 'life is not as bad as all that.' One might think he was carrying biblical history on his back, and the part a donkey played in it, of the hope for mankind that the donkey carried into Jerusalem. Fred, as he gloomily stands in a field, or with his back to a hedge in the rain, or in the warmth of the stable, appears to be reflecting upon the violence and envy and greed which has filled the world since that day a donkey carried Jesus into Jerusalem.

Do cats suffer from depression? They experience grief, like dogs, and of that I am sure. Ambrose is a witness to that. Ambrose pined for Oliver. Ambrose was at a loss for weeks without Oliver. In this practical age, it is considered foolish to believe that an animal can have emotions, but I am glad to be one of the foolish. I am certain that Monty, for instance, was angry when we lived our London night-life and left him alone; and that Lama was hurt when Oliver came on to the scene; and that Oliver himself felt vulnerable when he realised he had made his home with us too late in his life; and that Ambrose, from the moment he was born, has suffered from a distrust of the human race.

We, too, had a fear for him. There is always a fear, for instance, that a fox might catch a cat. It is the sort of fear which is automatic when one cares for a being, human or animal. 'Drive carefully,' one says to a friend, who is setting out on a journey. 'Be careful when you cross the road,' one says to a child. 'Keep the dog on the lead,' one says to another. The warning list is endless, as endless as the subconscious fears that a disaster awaits whenever a routine is broken.

I have twice seen Ambrose face to face with a fox. Each time I was scared for him; each time, however, my scare was unnecessary. On one occasion, I saw him wandering up the lane beyond Monty's Leap while a vixen was trotting down the lane towards him. A ginger cat facing a ginger-coloured vixen. But it was not Ambrose who turned and ran. It was the vixen.

Then there was another occasion when I heard a caterwauling coming from the hedge halfway down the donkey field between the cottage and the wood. I was up by the well at the time and so, by looking down the slope of the field, I could see what was happening. Ambrose was on the hedge, a fox on the grass below him. Ambrose was in a rage; the fox was cowering. A second later, the fox was away, running towards the wood while Ambrose, victory achieved, glared after him, then delicately began to wash a paw. Watching him, I remembered another time, years, years before, when I saw another ginger cat in the same field, fooling me momentarily into thinking I was watching a fox chase another; it was Monty who was doing the chasing.

Ambrose, therefore, is safe when he is alert. Unfortunately, like other cats, he is inclined to have a one-track mind and, when he suspects a mouse in a hedge or a patch of grass, he is oblivious to any danger that might threaten him. I had a scare the other day, for instance, when I saw a buzzard slowly wheeling above a field where Ambrose was ensconced outside a rabbit hole. I had never considered a buzzard a threat to a cat until a visitor told me a story of how a buzzard swept down and attacked her own cat. The cat survived, but only because of the skill of a vet. So, when I saw this buzzard hovering above a one-track-minded Ambrose, I rushed across the field clapping my hands and shouting.

It is, however, impossible to be a permanent guardian to a cat. A cat will be dozing, apparently content, in a corner of a garden, then suddenly disappear for hours, deaf to your calls, no sign of him in any of those haunts you know from past experience he favours. When Ambrose, double of Monty, disappears, I often have at the back of my mind an agonising occasion when Monty disappeared. It was a sunny May afternoon and Monty was dozing in the tiny garden outside the cottage door, and where Ambrose now often dozes. That afternoon, Monty proceeded to do the cat-vanishing trick . . . one moment dozing, the next nowhere to be seen. I had a sixth sense that he was in trouble. Normally I might have ignored his absence, accepting the fact that he would return in due course, but a warning bell was ringing in my ears. Just as well. I stood on a bank calling him then, suddenly, far across a field of young green corn, in a spot where I had never known Monty go before, I saw a gently flapping tail. It was a time when gin traps were still legal. Monty had been caught in one. We raced across the field, managed to release him and brought him back to the cottage, where he lay panting on the sofa.

No threat from a gin trap, therefore, for Ambrose; no threat from a snare, legal successor to the gin trap either, because our neighbouring farmers are reluctant to use it despite the current mass increase of rabbits. For the snare is even more vicious than the gin trap. The gin trap maims, but the snare strangles. A snare will be set outside a rabbit hole or across a rabbit track in a field. Any small animal can be caught in it; certainly a cat. My neighbouring farmers may be against using the cruelty of a snare but, like the human race, rabbits continue to multiply, continue to eat up the crops the farmer cannot afford to lose. Netting, I believe, offers the answer to the problem. The netting is pegged around the rabbit holes of an area, a ferret is sent down into the warren, and the rabbits are chased out into the netting and are speedily killed by the trapper.

Ambrose's danger, apart from his one-track mindedness, lay in the noise of the wind and the rustle of leaves hiding the sound of a fox's approach, or in a cat's capacity for profound sleep. I have often found Ambrose deep in an undergrowth corner, curled in a ball, oblivious of my presence and, although in the daytime this may not constitute a danger, it is worrying when he chooses to sleep outside during a warm summer night.

'Is Ambrose your side of the bed?' I will murmur, sleepily, to Jeannie.

'No.'

And in those early hours I will proceed to worry until I hear a noise at the window, followed by a gentle thump at the bottom of the bed. On other occasions, however, I have another worry. I hear the noise at the window, but there is no gentle thump on the bed. Instead there is a thump on the floor and I realise that Ambrose has by-passed the bed and hastened into the sitting room. Such behaviour often means he has brought us a present – a mouse, or a young rabbit perhaps. I lie there, wondering whether to get up and find out what the present might be. My only satisfaction is that I know it will never be a bird. Like Monty, Lama and Oliver, Ambrose has never been a cat who catches birds.

This particular May, a vixen was feeding her cubs in an earth down the cliff, close to a meadow where, in January, we had picked the first Magnificence daffodils. The earth had a beautiful setting, with an opening coming from under a stone hedge in an ancient, unused meadow. In summer, high bracken and the leaves of the brambles covered the entrance but, in May, there was a carpet of bluebells, cushions of white stitchwort, buttercups, sorrel and the deep pink flowers of the campion. Below, perhaps fifty feet below, was the sea surging against the rocks, creating a ribbon of foam, and there were gulls on the rocks, somnolent gulls, unsuspecting gulls ... for it seemed that this vixen and her family had a weakness for gulls. Outside the earth I discovered disregarded remnants of gulls.

But I also saw the vixen bring a rabbit to the cubs. It was a lucky moment with a strange aftermath. I had taken a stroll before breakfast and had slowly made my way along the narrow path through the cliff meadows until I reached the ivy-covered rock at the top of what we call the Folly Steps. The Folly Steps led down thirty feet or more to another sequence of meadows, including the meadow where we had picked the first Magnificence daffodils, which was close to the earth of the cubs. Indeed, the ivy-covered rock provided a perfect hideout from which to watch the cubs. I could look down at them at play without fear that they might spy me.

When I reached the rock, I saw no sign of the cubs. Nevertheless, I lingered there, staring out to sea, the salty breeze brushing my face, and idly watched three gannets diving a mile or two offshore. There was the backdrop of the Lizard stretching to the horizon on my left and, sailing westwards on the course taken by merchant ships between the Lizard and Land's End, was a single small coaster. The gannets were beautiful to watch. High above the quiet, deep blue sea, their giant wings outstretched, they roamed the sky until suddenly a fish was seen and they plummeted into the water, disappearing for a few seconds, then surfacing with their capture; another few moments while they gobbled it, then up to roam the sky again.

I had been sitting there on the ivy-covered rock for ten minutes before I saw the vixen. She was directly below me, emerging from a dense cluster of blackthorn a few yards from her earth and dangling from her mouth was a rabbit. She ran along the top of the hedge, then down among the bluebells, the white stitchwort, the buttercups, sorrel and the deep pink flowers of the campion and disappeared from view into the earth. I waited a little while longer, then slowly made my way back to the cottage, where I was greeted by an excited Jeannie.

'Oh, there you are,' she said, 'I've been longing to tell you what happened soon after you went. Ambrose and I were at Monty's Leap, when down the lane came a vixen with a rabbit dangling out of her mouth! Of course, she ran over into the field as soon as she saw us.'

'And I can tell you where she took it!' I replied.

There were other potential threats to Ambrose besides those that might come from foxes. Adders posed a threat. Monty once caught an adder, then dragged it, dead, into the cottage. I have seen Ambrose staring with fascination at an adder coiled in the grass under one of the apple trees. Cats may be quick in attack, but adders can be quicker. I have yet to see Ambrose catch an adder but, in July of this summer, he had an encounter with a stoat.

The first I knew of the encounter was a stench of a stoat one evening when Ambrose jumped on my lap as I sat in my corner of the sofa.

'Ugh!' I said, holding my nose. '*What* have you been up to, Ambrose?'

He was not pleased. He jumped off me, stalked to the door and demanded to be let out.

'Let him go!' I said to Jeannie, 'he stinks!'

She opened the door and Ambrose went out into the darkness.

He came back through the window after we had turned the lights out, missed out the bed and went into the sitting room. As always, I was glad he was home and I was soon asleep. At dawn, however, I was suddenly woken. Ambrose had jumped on the bed hissing and spitting and, when I dozily put out a hand to touch him, he leapt to the window and away. I should have been warned that something was amiss. Instead I went back to sleep.

At breakfast time he had not reappeared.

'I've got his fish for him,' said Jeannie. 'Funny that he hasn't come for it.'

'We'll go and have a search.'

We went outside and started calling. We called and called and there was no sign of him. An hour went by; two hours and then, to our joy, as we were standing on the bridge, he came round the corner by the *escallonia* ... but, instead of pausing beside us, he hurried past and into the field behind us.

71

'Did you notice his face?' Jeannie said. 'I thought it was a little puffed.'

'I don't think so,' I said, trying to reassure myself.

We did not see him again all day and evening came and there was still no sign of him and his plate of fish was untouched. When darkness fell, we were frantic. We each had a torch and off we went in different directions, calling into the night: 'Ambrose! Ambrose!'

How absurd, I thought, that in this world of turmoil I should be so concerned for a cat.

'Ambrose! Ambrose!'

We searched in ever-widening circles around the environment of the cottage. Across Monty's Leap and up the lane, down the path to Fred's field and the cliff meadows, up to the well and the field beyond, in every corner of the wood ... it was now one o'clock in the morning. He had not been seen for fourteen hours.

I had given up, ready to go to bed, when I flashed my torch under the veronica bush outside the bathroom.

'Found him!' I shouted to Jeannie. He was curled in a ball on dry leaves outside my reach. But my shout woke him up and, one glance at me, he ran away. I cursed myself. It was so foolish of me to shout. Once again, we could not find him and another hour went by. Then I said to Jeannie that, as he could run away so quickly and we now knew he was around, we could best leave him and have some sleep.

We were up at six, drops of rain were beginning to fall and there were thick clouds to the south coming in from the sea. I went round immediatley to the veronica bush in the hope that he might have returned there and indeed he had. He was once again curled on the still dry leaves and I moved cautiously towards him, then shot out a hand and grabbed him. He did not struggle.

I held him in my arms and the side of his face was puffed up into the size of a fist and he stank. Obviously he had lost his fight with the stoat.

'Teach you not to be so foolish,' I said. 'Now I'll have to phone the vet for you.'

We proceeded to take him down to the Orlyt, to his daybed in the Orlyt, a pile of last summer's bracken, gathered as winter bedding for the donkeys, but taken over by Ambrose, who had made comfortable dents in it. He would be safe and warm there and we shut the door so that he could not escape.

I had breakfast when I returned from telephoning and afterwards said to Jeannie that, as the vet would be out within the hour, we ought to collect Ambrose and bring him indoors. He was going to be a difficult patient, we knew that, and we also realised that unless one of us were holding him when the vet arrived, he would race away and hide.

So we went back to the Orlyt and opened its door. We looked at the daybed and it was empty. We looked at the whole length of the Orlyt and there was not a hint of his whereabouts. How could he have so vanished? The doors at both ends were shut. There was no open window for him to jump through.

Suddenly it dawned on me where he had gone.

At the far end of the Orlyt there was an oil-fired greenhouse heating machine which we no longer could afford to use because of the price of oil. On either side of the machine were large galvanised tunnel vents, through which the heat from the machine was distributed throughout the greenhouse by polythene tunnels.

I walked down to the galvanised vents and banged them with my hand. There was a shuffling noise inside. I banged the vents again; banged them harder and harder ... and then out of one of the exits dashed Ambrose. He did not seem to know us. He was like a mad cat. He raced away up to the other end of the Orlyt and began throwing himself against the glass. Then, when I went after him, Jeannie beside me making noises aimed to soothe him, he turned round and came at speed towards us before swerving into the patch of cucumber plants and their tendrils. He jumped his way through them and down the side of the greenhouse, back towards the galvanised vents. I had anticipated this. I had guessed he would try to return to the imaginary safety of their darkness, and I had blocked the exits. He was so thwarted when he discovered this that he lay down, panting, and this gave me the opportunity I required. I lunged forward like a rugby football tackler and caught him.

Soon afterwards the vet arrived. Jeannie met him as he drove up in his car and told him the story while I waited, fearing that Ambrose might explode into violent action when he saw the stranger.

The vet came quietly towards us.

'Hello, Ambrose,' he said quietly, 'we haven't met before, have we?'

There was no struggle in my arms; no movement. Ambrose was exhausted. He did not care what happened to him and there was not even a cry as the vet put the needle into him and gave him an injection.

We could see the bite, a tiny slit inside his mouth, and around it a balloon swelling from the poison. It must have been very painful and one could understand the wildness he had displayed.

'Keep him warm and quiet,' said the vet, 'and indoors, of course.'

I glanced at Jeannie.

'We'll try,' I said. 'We've never kept him indoors for long before.'

'Don't expect it will be for more than three days,' said the vet, 'and I'll be out to see him tomorrow.'

To our surprise, Ambrose proved an amiable patient. We kept him shut in the spare room, an earth-box ready for him, and he spent his time in the darkness under the bed. On the evening of the third day, the swelling in his mouth burst and the poison was got rid of, and within a day or two after that he was returning to his old self.

Naturally we rejoiced.

We were still rejoicing when, late one afternoon in the same week, Margaret, our friend from the pottery and our help during the daffodil season, arrived at the cottage with a beautiful greeny-brown jug which Jeannie had ordered from her. The two of them gossiped for a while and then, as Margaret was leaving, Jeannie happened to say, looking across to the moorland on the other side of the valley:

'Isn't the bracken lovely with the sun on it? Every day of

our lives Derek and I say how lucky we are to gaze on the land. In our minds we call it our own.'

There was a pause. Margaret was silent. Then she said:

'Didn't you know it is about to be sold? Didn't you see the Planning Application in last week's *Cornishman?*'

SIX

Curious how one responds to a time of crisis. A trivial crisis, a crisis which can be solved in a day, can evoke an explosion of anger or distress. A serious crisis, a crisis which can affect one's whole future, can evoke a kind of measured calmness.

'Let's go up to the bridge,' I said to Jeannie, as we watched Margaret's car disappear up the lane. 'There's no place better to talk about this shattering news.'

We walked up the path and turned left by the *escallonia*, and stood there looking across at the land on the other side of the valley. From that moment when we first came to Minack, the land we looked out upon had been a part of ourselves.

'Strange, isn't it?' said Jeannie, 'what the couple said to us this morning.'

The couple came every year to see us. They had followed the *Minack Chronicles* since their beginning.

'Yes,' I said, remembering how they had stood just where we were now standing, looking across at the moorland and the sweep of Mount's Bay. One of them said, as if it meant as much to them as to ourselves: 'You must always keep this view!'

'And now it may go.'

'Darling,' I said, my serious crisis calmness taking charge, 'we must collect the facts. First, let's find the *Cornishman* and find out about this Planning Application.'

The *Cornishman*, our local paper, is published on a Thursday and Jeannie collects it, along with daily papers on the Friday when she goes to Penzance. We do not, unless there is a special reason, have a daily paper on other days but, on Sundays, we collect the Sunday papers and their magazines.

77

When we have finished with these, we dump them in the flower house and they stay there, filling up space, until at last we have a burn. This is when we carry them and the contents of many weeks of filled waste-paper baskets, to a special place where we set them alight. It is surprising how often, the day after the burn, we urgently need to look at one of the waste-paper baskets.

I knew the *Cornishman* we required had not been burnt, but I had to look for the issue among the pile in the flower house and, when I found it, and when I read what we were looking for, I ran back to Jeannie in horror. My serious crisis calmness had vanished.

Under a notice headed PENWITH DISTRICT COUNCIL were the words 'The following applications for planning permission have been registered by the Council, and representations should be made within 14 days of the publication of this notice:

Mr E. J. Booth
Use of land for stationing agricultural caravan,
Rosemodress Farm, St Buryan.'

Rosemodress was the name of Bill's farm.

'It doesn't say exactly where on the land,' said Jeannie.

'But if Bill is selling the moorland, where else could it be except down here?'

'There's the lane. We built the lane. A stranger couldn't use the lane.'

'I simply cannot understand why we haven't been told about it. We have obviously been very stupid. Those strangers we have seen with Bill from time to time must have been potential buyers, including this Mr Booth himself. Who is he? I've never heard of him. And why didn't someone mention it to us? I mean, we're friends with them all, and we see them often. It's incredible.'

'So what do we do?'

At this moment I heard a car coming down the lane.

'Oh, hell,' I said, 'we can't see anyone now.'

The car paused at Monty's Leap, then came on past the barn and to a stop. Out stepped a dapper young man, whom I recognised, but had not met. I had heard he was a successful Birmingham businessman, who had bought property in Cornwall, including a cottage for holiday purposes nearby. I had also heard he was a true lover of Cornwall and wanted to settle in the county one day.

He walked hurriedly up the path.

'I've come to see you about this land which is being sold,' he said, wasting no time. 'A caravan on your doorstep is not going to be pleasant for you ... and also a cesspit.'

'How do you know about this?' I said.

'Margaret has just told me about your reaction and so I thought I would come and tell you all I know about it. You see, I am also interested in buying the land.'

I was bemused. Two hours ago I believed our lives were proceeding along regular lines, smoothly except for the usual day to day problems. Four o'clock in the afternoon at peace; six o'clock in turmoil.

'We didn't know anything about the land being sold,' I said.

'It's been on the market since April.'

'Since April?' It became stranger and stranger why no one had told us; why Bill himself had not told us.

'We live in a quiet world down here,' I said, trying to make a joke out of our ignorance.

'Anyhow, if I buy it,' said the man, 'I'll have a horse or two grazing on the two fields and, as for the rest, I'll just let it be as it is.'

He had been good enough to come and see us and tell us his plans; telling us that his plans were much pleasanter than those of the unknown Mr Booth. Indeed, he declared, 'I am putting all my cards on the table.'

By this time, however, adrenalin was rising within me; nothing to do with the visitor who had the kindness to tell me of his intentions and warn me of those of Mr Booth, but because I was thinking how sad it was after all these years of loving the land around Minack that Jeannie and I were about to be cheated of it.

We were now sitting at the table in the porch, the man opposite me and Jeannie hovering by the door.

'I must ask you a personal question,' I said. 'Have you any idea what this land we're talking about means to Jeannie and me? I mean, have you read any of my books in which I have written about it?'

'No, I haven't read any of your books.'

As he spoke, I thought how miraculous it was that, despite his unawareness, he had taken the trouble to come specially to see us. In return, I believed I should try to convey exactly how I felt; how Jeannie felt.

'I think I should tell you,' I said, looking at him across the table and speaking very slowly, 'that I ... will ... fight ... for ... this ... land ... like ... a ... wild ... bull.'

A muddled simile perhaps, but it was reflecting my mood.

We said goodbye, and we watched his car disappear up the lane.

'We're in trouble,' I said.

'Deep trouble.'

'It reminds me of that day when we walked down the long, long road to see Harry Laity. The road seemed endless and, as we walked, we were aware that our whole future depended upon how we were received at the end of it. Had he refused to let us have Minack, what would have happened to us?'

'And what will happen to us now if a stranger gets hold of that land?' said Jeannie. 'You know how all sorts of building can be put up in the name of agriculture. Our isolation will be finished.'

We had moved into the cottage and had poured ourselves drinks, and I had sat down in my corner of the sofa when Ambrose appeared, looked up at me, made a miniature yap, thought about coming on my lap, changed his mind, scratched for a moment on the chintz of Jeannie's chair, then leapt first on the arm and then onto her lap.

'Comforting,' said Jeannie, stroking his back with a finger. 'You're always comforting, Ambrose.'

He responded by purring, twisting his head, looking up at her face.

'This may be a crisis,' I said. 'Maybe one of the biggest in our lives, but we ought to keep it in perspective. We might have had news there was to be a nuclear power station, a housing estate, a motorway. Those sorts of crises are happening all over the world to people.'

'But,' said Jeannie, 'it's all relative, isn't it? A caravan on our doorstep with strangers living in it would be equivalent to any of those threats you mention as far as we are concerned.'

'Let's plan what we're going to do,' I said, changing the subject to practical matters.

'Why not go to see Bill?'

'Tonight? Too late. And anyhow, we must get all the facts before we see him. We must go to the estate agency and get the sale details, and we must go to the Council Offices and look at the plans which Mr Booth has lodged there. Presumably he hasn't completed the sale because he doesn't know whether his plans will be passed. That's why our friend just now was so confident. He knows the offer of sale is still open.'

'What about the price?' said Jeannie, still stroking Ambrose.

'Don't think of that at this moment,' I laughed. 'We can't afford it whatever the price, but that's not the point. We have to find out exactly how many acres are involved and whether we can compete with these other two. We may be too late. All I know is that if we have a chance to buy it, we *have* to do so, however many banks we have to rob.'

We decided to go to bed early, before darkness fell, because we suddenly felt the strain of the evening events and, in the morning, we would be off early on our investigations. First, however, I had to check up that the donkeys were all right and, when I went outside, a drizzly rain was falling. I had reached the gate by the barn when I saw four teenage girls coming up the path from the direction of the coastal path and, when I greeted them, I found they were German, walking round Cornwall, sleeping in tents.

It was nearly dusk and they did not ask to pitch their tents near us, but they asked if I would fill their flasks with water. This I proceeded to do. They were so polite, and charming, and grateful, that I said they could come back in the morning if they so wished and wash and have a breakfast out of the drizzly rain. It was one of those invitations which one regrets next day.

I awoke the following day with the realisation of the full enormity of the crisis. The previous evening I had been able to talk with adrenalin flowing and coping with the situation seemed possible. Now it dawned on me that the price for the land might be so high that it would be far, far out of our reach however accommodating the bank might be and, anyhow, since our Birmingham friend now knew we were also in the race, he would be aiming to come to a quick decision. Or perhaps the mysterious Mr Booth had paid for an option on the land, pending the decision on the planning application? So many imponderables and we needed to be alone to concentrate upon them. Neither of us, therefore, rejoiced at the thought of greeting four young German girls, whose English was limited, at breakfast time on a drizzly, foggy morning.

However, by half past eight they appeared, cheerful despite the rainy night they had spent in their tent, and I led them into the flower house and soon Jeannie arrived with boiled eggs, homemade bread and butter and a large pot of tea. Naturally I would have preferred them to have left as soon as possible because we had now laid our plans as to what we were going to do that morning ... but the girls lingered on. In retrospect, I am glad they held us up. There was time to achieve a *rapport* and, last Christmas, we were given a tangible memory of their visit and of that crucial day of our lives. One of the girls had written to us after they returned to Germany from their holiday, and we had kept up a correspondence ever since. Last Christmas, a parcel arrived from her, an elaborate parcel containing a tin with air-holes pierced in the top of it. The parcel contained a feathery leaf plant which the girl had grown from a seed. It now stands in a pot, also of her own making, in the porch.

When the girls left, we put our plans into action. First we drove to Penzance and to the estate agent, who was handling the sale. We collected the details and the map that went with it, and found out that thirty-seven acres were for sale, of which eighteen acres represented the land on the other side of the valley. The remaining nineteen acres were farm land, as opposed to moorland and, of course, to buy such land would be financially out of the question. Thus we had achieved our first objective. Whatever the situation might be, we now knew that we could only be successful if the sale were split into two sections: someone to buy the farm land; ourselves to buy the moorland.

Next we set off for the Council Offices to see the planning application that Mr Booth had made. A courteous clerk produced it from a folder, laid it out on a table and waited for my reaction.

The planning application requested permission for a caravan, water supplies, and a cesspit in the corner of the field within thirty yards of Monty's Leap.

Mr Booth, apparently, came from Ireland. He planned to breed bees.

The courteous clerk was watching my face, and he soothed me when he saw it becoming bucolic by saying that he did not think the application would be approved, adding the kind of remark one needs in a moment of distress. He said that Minack was a special place and so it would be foolish to see it spoilt. The local parish council, on the other hand, were not to share his view. When, at the first stage of the application curriculum they were asked their opinion, they unanimously approved the planning application of Mr Booth.

We left the Council Offices and set off for Falmouth. We were going there because a friend of mine called Michael Williams had told me that if ever I was in serious trouble, there was a solicitor in Falmouth who would have the quickness of mind to understand me. My friend Michael Williams was a schoolmaster when I first knew him. Then he and his wife bought a small hotel near Tintagel and, although they had had no previous hotel experience, they proceeded to make it one of the most successful on the north Cornish coast. The way they welcomed their guests was the secret. A warm welcome, an easy-going atmosphere, is always the way to success of a small hotel. In due course, they sold their hotel and Michael set out to achieve an ambition which had always haunted him. He began a publishing business, Bossinney Books, which concentrates on publications dealing mostly with Cornwall and Devon. They are admirably produced and their subjects cover every aspect of these two counties. Anyone interested in Cornwall and Devon should set out to collect the publications of Bossinney Books.

I had made a note of the solicitor's name when Michael mentioned it two or three years before and had waited. I sensed that a critical moment would come when I would need him, and it had now arrived. We were, therefore, on the road to Falmouth, speeding along, hoping that the solicitor was not away, or in Court, or was so full up with appointments that he would not be able to see us. We were in luck. He was there. He was free and, within a few minutes of arriving at his offices, we were telling him our story, and when we left we had the comfortable feeling that we had an ally on whose help and advice we could rely. He was, however, as puzzled as we were that no one had told us that the land was for sale. The only way to solve this mystery was to pay a call on Bill, the farmer whose land it was. That evening I did so.

I had not relished the thought of it. I am not by nature a businessman; someone who possesses the instinct how to carry through a deal. I am, for instance, one of those people who prefer to give something away rather than haggle over a price. Jeannie is one of those people too. Neither of us, in fact, has any joy in looking for bargains, because we are thinking of those who are the sufferers. Partly this stems from our experience of daffodil bargains. The media may proclaim, for instance, that daffodil prices are very cheap for the buying public ... Jeannie and I know what that means for the producer.

I found Bill in his garden.

I mentioned the weather, I asked how his tomato plants were growing; idle talk to soften the purpose of my visit.

'Bill,' I then said, 'I've just heard that you're selling the land our way; the moorland on the other side of the valley.'

He looked at me in astonishment.

'You've just heard? You didn't know anything about it?'

'No, Bill.'

'I put the advertisement in the *Cornishman* in April. Didn't you see the advertisement?'

I explained that I seldom pored through the advertisements. There were so many houses and properties for sale, and there was no reason for me to read about them.

'When we didn't hear from you,' he said, 'we thought you weren't interested.' Then he added: 'And there haven't been any bones for the dogs lately. Thought perhaps you didn't want to see us.'

Bones for the dogs? Had our future depended upon bones for the dogs?

'Bill,' I said, 'the only reason why there haven't been bones for the dogs is that we've been having topside and not lamb!'

The tone of the conversation was obviously a relief to me. There are times when I have suffered from a form of persecution mania, when I have interpreted some action, or

lack of action, on somebody's part, as a veiled attack on me. It is, I suppose, commonplace for people to suffer like that occasionally. The most usual example is when somebody you know appears to avoid you, passing you in the street without stopping, or failing to talk to you at some gathering. You worry about it afterwards, wondering why you have been ignored, yet the explanation is probably quite simple. No offence had been meant.

No offence had been intended on the part of Bill or ourselves. It was a misunderstanding which can breed more misunderstandings. We feared he had not told us about the sale because he did not want us to have the land. He thought, because we had not seen the advertisement, because we had been having topside instead of lamb, that we were not interested in acquiring the land. I left him, therefore, feeling soothed. He had not barred us from the race for the land.

'You know what to do,' he said, and then added as I was

leaving him, 'mind, the application for the caravan is eighty percent certain to be approved!'

I guessed what he meant. He was saying that we could go ahead in the battle for the land, but that he was still a businessman expecting a fair price. That, I think, was the message I took away from that meeting. He wanted a fair price, not an exorbitant one. He was a deep-rooted Cornishman, who would like to preserve a section of Cornwall's heritage if it were possible.

Jeannie and I now had luck on our side. There are some times when the jigsaw pieces of one's good intentions refuse to fit. Something outside one's control interferes with one's hopes. I remember such situations when I was young and pursuing girls. I would have a date, and I would be delayed at the office, and when I arrived at the meeting place she was not there. Or the times when I was a reporter pursuing a story and all those I wished to interview had just gone out and could not be found. Legions of incidents I can remember, where the jigsaw pieces of my good intentions refused to fit. But, as I said, luck for Jeannie and me was now on our side.

The agent of the Falmouth Estate, the landlords of Minack, paid a surprise visit to us. He too had known nothing about the land being for sale, but he straightaway showed interest in the nineteen acres of farming land which, in any case, we would not be able to buy. He said he would seriously go into the matter. Meanwhile, I had contacted our solicitor, told him of my conversation with Bill, and asked him to get in touch with the estate agents responsible for the sale.

Now began that period of waiting which sellers or buyers of property have to become accustomed to.

'Anything in the post?'

'Nothing.'

'Why not go and telephone?'

'This afternoon when I take the tomatoes in.'

I take the tomatoes in and come back.

'I got the secretary. No one was in to give me any news.'

Two days, three days, four days … waiting.

One morning we caught sight of our Birmingham friend on the other side of the valley. He had a man with him wearing a cap and he was walking around the fields, a map in his hands.

'He hasn't given up,' I said,

'What people don't understand,' said Jeannie, 'is what that land *means* to us. It is our whole life. Maybe that is being sentimental, but it's true. Other people buy property just because it is property. We're wanting to buy that land because it represents to us a kind of magic. We're not being sensible in that we are thinking of it as an investment or that sort of thing. We are wanting to buy the view, buy the safety of not seeing another part of Cornwall being rationalised. It is a dream we are wanting to buy.'

The price for the dream was about to be revealed to us. Our solicitor had received his instructions from the estate agency dealing with the sale. The price for the eighteen acres was several thousands of pounds.

'It's a terrible amount,' said Jeannie.

'We know there are at least two people after it.'

'How possibly can we raise the money?'

'Lloyds Bank have always been kind to us … and you know Lloyds will be aware we have the backing of those people who read my books. Without them there would not be a chance of raising the money.'

'A nice thought.'

'But, of course, we will have to bargain.'

'Of course we must,' said Jeannie.

It was at this stage that we had another piece of luck. In retrospect, probably the most important piece of luck of all.

Three weeks previously and, thus, long before there was any hint of our problem, Ron Messum the accountant of the CGA wrote to us that he would be on holiday in Cornwall and that he would call on us. The initials CGA stand for the Country Gentlemen's Association; an old fashioned name for these days, though the Association is very up to date in its methods. I joined it some years ago and it has been of help to me on many occasions in many different ways. In particular, it has been of special help regarding financial affairs and two of those who have been of special help have been Ron Messum and Ken Raw.

It so happened that Ron Messum arrived at the cottage on the very morning that I had been told of the price of the land. I led him indoors, and he sat down on the sofa which had been a part of so many crucial stages of my life, and I proceeded to tell him the full story, from the moment we had heard the land was for sale to this present moment when we had decided to make an offer.

His reaction startled me.

'Make an offer?' he said. 'Crazy thing to do!'

'Why?' I said.

'Don't you realise you'll start an auction? You've got two people for sure who are rivalling you. You've been asked for a firm price ... but, if you start bargaining, the estate agent will go back to the others and the auction will start. And from what you tell me, they've got the money ... and before you know where you are the price will go right out of your reach. So, just in order to try saving a few hundred, you will lose the land.'

He paused.

'Now,' he said, and he was fumbling in his pocket, 'here's 10p ... go out at once to the nearest telephone kiosk and tell your solicitor that you accept the price.'

'What about getting the money for it?'

'Don't worry about that now. The bank will lend it to you ... but you get the land first!'

I obeyed him.

I went to the garage, backed the car out, and drove to the telephone kiosk at the hamlet of Sheffield on the way to Penzance. I put Ron Messum's 10p in the slot, pressed the coin when I heard the answering voice ... and twenty minutes later I was back in the cottage.

'Jeannie,' I said, Ron Messum still sitting on the sofa, now sipping a glass of wine, 'I believe we are about to become landowners!'

At 4 p.m. we *were* landowners.

I had telephoned the solicitor again. The price had been agreed.

That evening we had a date at the village hall in Lamorna to hear a concert by the Lamorna Singers and by a friend of ours, Malcolm Sutton, the pianist.

On the way, we met Bill in the lane, and I stopped and got out of the car. There was a smile on his face and he held out his hand, and he said:

'It's yours. I'm glad!'

Then he added, mischievously:

'The other two, you know, were right on your tail!'

SEVEN

We were still not safe. In theory we might have become the owners of the moorland, but we still had to raise the money to pay for it; and there still lay ahead the legal rigmarole, which could easily present problems.

'Jeannie, are we crazy?'

'In some people's opinion . . . yes, I am sure.'

I was leaning against the stone wall of the bridge, half-sitting on the blue slates that lined the top of it, the deep, rose-pink flowers of the burgeoning *escallonia* bush humming with bees on my right. Jeannie was opposite me, sitting on the step which led to the meadow where the Joseph McLeod daffodils grew, their foliage now dying back and being smothered by a forest of grasses. A bottle of dry white wine stood on the garden table between us, and I picked it up and filled her glass, then mine.

'Their opinion would be right too,' I said. 'I mean, here we are, buying eighteen acres of moorland which have no practical value whatsoever, while continuing to live in a cottage which we do not own and in circumstances which, let's face it, few people would put up with.'

Jeannie looked at me, smiling, the wine glass cupped in her hands:

'We could have had the bedroom added on with the money we are going to spend.'

Jeannie had long wanted a bedroom in which there was space.

'You know,' I said, 'when you come to think of it . . . all the years we have been here have been like camping.

'A little exaggeration.'

'By today's standards, I mean. As you say, take the bedroom ...'

The floor space of the bedroom was fifty square feet.

'Who would put up with a bedroom like ours?'

'Yes, I would like a big bedroom.'

Jeannie's plan has always been to build such a bedroom at the other end of the cottage where the spare bedroom and bathroom jut into the donkey field. The spare bedroom was bought as a chicken house and we transformed it, panelling the sides and ceiling with hardboard, then covering the ceiling with Werner Graf wallpaper and painting the sides white. The outside of the chicken-house was disguised by

cedarwood shingles. Jeannie's plan was to build a granite-walled room on the other side of the bathroom, a spacious bedroom with a magnificent view facing the expanse of Mount's Bay.

'A big bedroom or eighteen acres of moorland,' I said. 'A curious choice to make. Material comfort or the continuation of a dream.'

Ambrose appeared round the corner by the *escallonia*.

'Ambrose, you are extraordinary,' said Jeannie. '*How* did you know we were here?'

It always charmed us, this Ambrose trick of suddenly appearing as we sat at this place we called the bridge.

'Ten minutes ago,' added Jeannie, 'I saw him in the flower house, fast asleep. Too far away to hear us talking.'

Ambrose gave one of his little yaps, then jumped up beside me and, as I stroked him, I turned round so that I was now looking out across to the moorland and to Carn Barges and to the sea beyond.

'Fantastic, isn't it?' I said, 'that we stood at Carn Barges those years ago, gazing for the first time towards this cottage, a ginger cat in our lives then ... a ginger cat in our lives now.'

'The present ginger cat was talking to his friend this morning.'

'Where?'

'Up the lane the other side of the Leap.'

'Noddy, I suppose.'

'Yes.'

Noddy was a huge, white cat, so huge that Ambrose by comparison resembled a small cat. Noddy came from the Phillips' farm a couple of miles away, from where we buy our eggs; eggs that have the flavour of old-fashioned farm eggs. Noddy was a roamer and, from time to time, he would choose our area of land in which to hunt, and we would see him in a corner of some field crouched in anticipation as he waited for a rabbit to appear. Since white, in rabbit language, is a signal of danger, only foolish rabbits could have been Noddy's victims. For, as he crouched waiting, he looked like a giant white pillow.

As for his friendship with Ambrose, it was never close. It was one of those cat friendships in which two cats stare at each other at a respectful distance, saying little, as far as a human ear can tell, and therefore seeming to be communicating with each other on an ESP basis. Of course, if Jeannie or I appeared, Ambrose would change his attitude towards Noddy, and he would erupt into an explosion. The huge white Noddy would be despatched off the premises by the fierce ginger cat of Minack.

That summer, after Oliver died, we had been half hoping that a successor might arrive who would be acceptable to Ambrose. The first such possible candidate, as I have already described, was speedily sent spitting by Ambrose. The next such candidate (Noddy was never a candidate because he had such a good home that he would never have dreamt of leaving it) gave Jeannie and me much excitement. For the candidate was black; all black from nose tip to tail tip ... exactly resembling Lama and Oliver.

We first saw this little black cat when we were walking up the lane to fetch the milk from the farm. It was thirty yards ahead, coming jauntily towards us.

'Jeannie,' I said, 'I can't believe it!'

He caught sight of us and dived into the hedge and out of sight.

'Ssh!' said Jeannie, 'stay here.'

Jeannie, being by birth a cat lover, possessing the confidence of such a person, proceeded to walk up the lane calling: 'Puss! Puss!' ... and expressing coo noises which, in her view, would prove irresistible to the little black cat who had run away.

To no avail.

'It can't be Walter's,' she said, returning to me. 'Walter has never had a black cat.'

Walter Grose, Pied Piper of cats, was joint farmer with our

friend Jack Cockram of the farm from which we collected our milk, and who, at that time, was always surrounded by cats as he sat in his yellow van at midday eating his crust.

'He has only mongrel cats,' I said.

We were intrigued, naturally, for if a third black cat came into our lives uninvited it would truly be a miracle.

Two mornings later, Jeannie came rushing into the cottage, calling: 'Where are the field-glasses? Quick!'

The field-glasses were on the sofa and I picked them up and gave them to her.

'Fergus is down by the Leap, just sitting there!'

'Fergus?' I said, following her out.

'Yes. Fergus, the black cat.'

'Jeannie,' I said, 'this cat hasn't got a name. We've only seen him once before.'

'I've christened him Fergus. It suits him.'

Now Jeannie did not say this in an authoritative tone. She said it as if it were the most normal step to take. A cat was coming into our lives and so no time must be wasted in giving it a name.

'Fergus,' I murmured to myself. 'How did such a name come to her?'

Fergus, it would seem, was testing us out, inspecting our qualifications. We saw him, off and on, for the next month and sometimes we would see him coming down the lane; sometimes crossing the stable meadow; sometimes I found him trotting busily past the flower house into the wood ... and on each occasion we caught the impression that he was a confident little cat, sure of himself, sure of the kind of home he was looking for. But where had he come from? What was leading him to haunt the tracks of Lama and Oliver?

At no time, however, did we see a meeting between him and Ambrose. Of course, although he might, when on his own, have had great confidence in himself, such confidence might quickly have been dissipated if he had been suddenly confronted by a cat who had no intentions of being polite.

Eventually, in fact, it was not to be Ambrose who drove him away from Minack. I was to drive him away. An incident took place in which I behaved very foolishly.

Jeannie had asked me to cut the grass under the washing line. It is a washing line which has a beautiful view, perhaps the most beautiful view of any washing line in the country. It stands fifty yards above the cottage close to our well, and as you are pegging the clothes on the line you can look up and see the whole sweep of Mount's Bay. It also has another advantage. The sea winds dry the clothes on the line and so, when they are brought back to the cottage, a handkerchief, a shirt, or a sheet, they have a soothing, soft, sea scent. The washing line, on the other hand, can also cause problems. After one gale, for instance, I collected several articles which had been hanging on the line in the next door field where my neighbour's cows were grazing.

I had started to cut the grass when the engine of the mower spluttered and stopped. I cursed myself for forgetting to fill up with petrol and set off down the path to collect the petrol can from the tractor shelter. When I reached the shelter, the can was not there, and I remembered I had left it beside the rotovator which I had been using earlier in the Orlyt. I walked into the Orlyt ... and saw, half way down, sitting in the wheelbarrow, calmly looking at me, Fergus.

Unfortunately, I was not as calm as he was. My instant reaction was to find Jeannie so that she could see for herself the astonishing sight of a black cat once again in the Orlyt, so I ran out, shutting the door, and calling for her at the top of my voice. It was idiot behaviour for, by the time I found Jeannie and we had returned, Fergus was at the far end of the Orlyt looking thoroughly startled; and when we walked down towards him he dashed up the other side of the greenhouse and hit himself against the glass at the end which we had just left. I ran back and opened the door and, a few seconds later, he was out and away.

96

There was a sequel to this story. Margaret and George, who kept the pottery at the end of our lane, had an elderly cat which, at this time, died. Not long afterwards, Fergus began to haunt *their* cottage and very soon he had nudged his way in, thus filling the vacancy. We have often seen him since; a squat, black little figure, so like Lama and Oliver, trotting up and down the end of the lane, and sometimes we have felt nervous for him. The end of the lane is much used and the main road is only a stone's throw from the home he has adopted.

Are we sure that the black cat who entered George and Margaret's home was the same black cat of the Orlyt? During the period that 'Fergus' was visiting us, I met the wife of a farmer who lived not far away.

'I've noticed,' she said, 'that our black cat Nancy has been going in your direction.'

Was Fergus, after all, Nancy? Was it Nancy we had been seeing all the time, and who was the black cat I had scared in the Orlyt?

I think not . . . for, after the Orlyt incident, after the entry of Fergus into the home of George and Margaret, we never saw a black cat at Minack again.

Incidents like this are so trivial against the background of world events. Yet it is the collection of trivial incidents that help to create the fabric of our lives. Without them our lives would be barren. Often we may be mesmerised by great events, great theories, great indignations, but frequently these are inspired by a kind of mass hysteria. In such situations, we do not belong to ourselves; we belong to a manipulated herd. We become insensitive to the trivial incidents, sad or happy, superficial or deep, which fill our lives with meaning.

Ambrose, we had now begun to realise, did not wish for a companion. There could be no possible replacement for Oliver. Oliver had brought him up and had been his only companion. There could be no substitute. Instead, I realised, he would depend more and more upon Jeannie and myself; and I, as a one time anti-cat person, as a person who still possessed a subconscious resentment against a cat exploiting me, was apprehensive.

I had an ally in Fred. Fred, during his life at Minack, had been apprehensive first of Lama, then of Oliver, then of Ambrose. Penny, when she first came to Minack and before she gave birth to Fred, however, had a friendship with Lama. Lama used to rub herself against Penny's hind leg and there was no fear on our part that Penny might take objection. Fred, on the other hand, was born like me with a suspicion of cats and, although I was converted to the charms of them, Fred has never been converted.

Thus, if Ambrose visits a meadow in which Fred is grazing, Fred will look questioningly at Ambrose, then lower his head and advance menacingly. There have been other times when Ambrose has become ensconced in the pile of bracken we keep in the stable for winter bedding, and Fred has entered the stable. I have seen Ambrose watch Fred carefully, and then, at an appropriate moment when he believes Fred is not looking, Ambrose will scurry out through the doorway. I would like them to be friends. I would like them to provide that cosy kind of picture in which you see a donkey and a cat in a stable together. But it is not to be.

Ambrose indoors, curled on the bed, has on occasions been an invaluable watch-cat as far as Fred and Merlin are concerned. The other night, for instance, I was woken up by the sound of Ambrose growling, followed by his jump to the window, followed by the crunching of footsteps on the stone chippings outside. I realised what had happened. The donkeys were out. The donkeys, soon after midnight, were loose in the garden.

They have a Houdini gift of getting out of the places in which they should have been placidly content. That night, thanks to Ambrose sounding the alarm, and thanks to the new battery I had just bought for the torch, I was able, in my dressing-gown, to corral the donkeys and manoeuvre them back through the gate they had succeeded in unlatching. On other occasions, when the watch-cat has not been on guard, I have had most unfortunate experiences.

For instance, one early summer morning, Ambrose, deep in sleep on the bed, did not hear the crunching sound of donkey steps on the stone chippings; and nor did I. Hence it was not until after breakfast that I suddenly found the donkeys were not where they should have been, and were, instead, in the vegetable garden.

When I discovered them roaming among the vegetables that not only were intended for current consumption but, far more importantly, were planned to keep us fed with vegetables through the winter, I was very angry with them indeed. I cursed Fred for being a greedy, selfish donkey, who had no consideration for the two people who cared for him and, as I did so, there was a phrase knocking at the back of my mind which sounded familiar, a phrase sometimes used in daily life: 'You don't appreciate what we do for you.'

On this particular occasion, when Fred and Merlin did their Houdini act, it was only in one corner of the vegetable garden that they had committed irretrievable damage. When I saw what they had done, I ran back to the cottage, calling for Jeannie.

'My onions!' I cried out, 'they've rolled on my onions! My onions are flattened!'

We were still waiting. Deeds were being examined and rumours developed. Jeannie met someone in Penzance who said they had heard a caravan site was to be 'your way'. Word came to us that the Falmouth Estate had changed their minds and were not going to buy the other acres for sale . . . and that now a property dealer was offering Bill two thousand pounds an acre for all the land. Bill had given us his word. We trusted him. But who could blame him if a developer offered him a price far beyond what we would be able to pay?

'No nesting swallows this year,' I said gloomily to Jeannie one day after the post had arrived and there was no news.

For five consecutive years there had been swallows at Minack, and they had made their mud nests and brought up their young, either in the old stables or in the so-called garage. Not a sign of a swallow inspecting either this summer, let alone building a nest.

'You're thinking what I've been thinking,' said Jeannie. 'Swallows bring good luck.'

'And this summer they are not bringing it.'

'Yes.'

'Oh, hell!' I said. 'We're getting too involved. We need a break.'

We were to get such a break. A letter arrived the following morning from Sir Hugh Wontner, Chairman of the Savoy Hotel Group, Jeannie's one-time chief, inviting us both to a celebration of the Savoy Hotel's ninetieth birthday. It was a delightful compliment for Jeannie. Those who have worked for any length of time with the Savoy Hotel Group develop a loyalty to it which some high-powered hoteliers find difficult to understand. Anyone like myself is only too able to understand it. I have been to a long sequence of restaurants and hotels where I have sat patiently while some member of the staff has approached Jeannie with the words: 'I was at the Savoy' ... and then Savoy stories rolled.

Jeannie, under her maiden name of Jean Nicol, wrote *Meet Me At The Savoy* soon after we first came to Minack. After an interval, she began writing a trilogy of novels, the story of which is a luxury London hotel and those who work in it. The story spans many years and, as a consequence, it reflects the contemporary scene of those years. *Hotel Regina* and *Home Is The Hotel* reflect the forties; the third of the trilogy takes the story to the seventies and is called *Bertoni's Hotel*. When the first two were published they were likened to Arnold Bennett's *Imperial Palace*, while a reviewer on the BBC said they were 'Incomparably better than Vicki Baum's *Grand*

Hotel.' It is a tribute to her that people write to her as if the characters in the novels were live people. One such character is Bertioni, general manager of the *Hotel Regina*, whose creed is to maintain the highest standards of service in his hotel. The other day Jeannie had a letter from a New Zealand admirer in which the writer said he had recently visited a one-time luxury hotel which had been taken over by a chain of hotels. 'I thought of Bertioni when I saw how the standards had been lowered,' he said. 'He would never have allowed it to happen!'

We stayed one night at the Savoy and, when we were invited to stay for another night, we explained that we had left our cat on his own at home and must return; so we left London at 7 p.m. and were back at Minack in the early hours of the morning.

Many people find it difficult to understand this sentimental loyalty some of us have for a dog or a cat left at home, or in a kennels, or in a cattery. I find it difficult to understand myself. After all, the cat or the dog is probably thankful to be left on its own. None of that fussing; none of that being picked up and hugged; none of that being taken for a walk when there was no wish for such a walk. Hence, it may be conceit on anyone's part to believe that they are being sadly missed, and so perhaps it was foolish of Jeannie and me to surrender another night at the Savoy in order to return to the company of a cat.

However, there was a special reason to do so now. Normally, on the rare occasions when we go away, Margaret comes morning and evening to see the donkeys and to feed Ambrose. She was not available this time. Thus Fred, Merlin and Ambrose had been left in sole charge of Minack and, as it was August, there was the risk of holidaymakers taking advantage of our absence and nosing around and scaring, if not the donkeys, Ambrose. Of course, before we had left for the comfort of the Savoy Hotel, there had been careful preparations and thus there were five saucers left in a row for

Ambrose. Fish, chopped lamb, chopped beef, milk and one of water; a menu which we hoped would suit any mood. On our return, in that early morning, we found when we entered the cottage that all the saucers, except the one containing water, were empty. Thus our catering plans had brought satisfaction. Where, however, was Ambrose?

His absence vexed us rather than worried us. We had returned specially to be with him; preferred a manifestation of love for him rather than another night in the Savoy . . . and he did not show any signs of wishing to greet us.

I must now explain the routine of what happens when Jeannie and I return to Minack after a day, or three days. If we have been to London, by the time we reach Exeter on the way home, I will begin to hear murmurs from my companion in the Volvo: 'Hold on, Ambrose, we won't be long now!' Such murmurs proceed to infect me and, by the time we have reached Bodmin Moor, I find that I myself am also murmuring, my foot steps on the accelerator: 'Hold on, Ambrose!'

Thus, when the journey is ending and we turn off the tarmac road into our own lane, and we drive along the rough surface, the headlights swathing round the turnings, the murmurings of my companion in the Volvo tend to switch to a call that exclaims: 'Ambrose! We are home!'

Hence, if Ambrose is not there to greet us; if, in fact, we have to wait ten minutes, twenty minutes, half an hour, before he deigns to come through the door we have left open for him, we are naturally disappointed; then irritated.

Clearly we were sentimental idiots to believe that he had missed us. We had been the victims of our own wish to love; an indulgent wish that cool-minded people would decry. Indifference, they might reasonably argue, is more realistic than yielding to emotion.

At that moment, I would have been ready to agree. Not, however, as dawn was breaking and I put out a hand and touched soft fur and listened to a steady stream of purrs.

The postman arrived in the morning, travelling in his little red van. We have always been lucky in our postmen. There were the Gilbert brothers, first Jim the stonemason, then Jack the cobbler. There was Willie Lugg and pretty Joan Payne and each, in their time, sorted the mail at St Buryan post office, then set off on their rounds by bicycle.

Computer efficiency changed this. Part-time postmen were dispensed with and we no longer see bicycles coming down the winding lane with our post. Instead little red vans from Penzance roam the district with the mail, and yet the mood of the bicycle postmen, the charming intimacy, has not changed.

Des is one of our postmen; Tony is another; and they will arrive at Minack after gossipy talks on their rounds, and Des may say to me: 'Sorry, only two bills for you today!' Or: 'You're popular ... look at the letters I'm bringing you.' Or Tony will ask: 'Anything to go?' Meaning ... is there anything which we want posted.

On this particular morning, among the letters was a bulky envelope which I did not open at once because I thought it only contained a magazine which someone had sent me. When, finally, I did so and saw the contents I pretended they were unimportant, saying nothing, handing them across the table for Jeannie to see. I wanted to see the happiness of her reaction. The Deeds had arrived for our inspection and included, of course, was the map of our boundaries.

I have never been a person who has been frightened by nostalgia. Some people want to put a wall round memories, and there are some who seem to think it bad manners to remember the past, and there are others who like to denigrate nostalgia. I do not understand their attitude. Why should it be wrong to recall the past? It is strange that if you wish to be considered conventional you must only concentrate on the present, however difficult present circumstances might be.

However, when Jeannie and I looked at the map, we had

pleasure in indulging in nostalgia for several reasons. One of them, for instance, was that the sea end of the far boundary of our new land included the very spot on Carn Barges where we stood and first saw across the moorland the small, grey stone cottage which was Minack. We were on holiday, wandering the district, half-hoping we might find a home to which we could retreat from London, and we had walked along the track from Lamorna Cove, then up the steep climb to the huge standing stone called Carn Barges. I remember a buzzard was sailing slowly in the blue June sky high above us, and I remember Jeannie's excited voice as she pointed inland: 'There it is!' At that instant, had we but known it, we had changed the course of our lives.

The first part of the donkey walk was also outlined on the map. When first we took Penny and Fred along it, there was only a track. It is still virtually a track in high summer when the bracken and brambles are high beside it and before Council workmen have had time to cut them down ... but now, of course, it is the Cornwall Coastal Path. On the seaward side, below the tangled undergrowth and trees, there was another reason for nostalgia.

Jutting out into the sea is a rocky promontory with a rock on it so carved by centuries of raging seas that it resembles a polar bear, and so close in similarity is it to a polar bear that it would have been appropriate if the promontory had been so named. Instead, it has the beautiful sounding name of Gazell. It has always fascinated me as to how sections of coastal regions received imaginative, romantic names. Who was it who walked the cliffs, pencil in hand, dreaming up a name like Gazell? In this case, the person must have passed the promontory at high tide. For, in giving it the name of Gazell, he also marked it down (since at the time it was cut off from the mainland by the high tide) as an island.

Thus we found from the Deeds that we were to possess an island.

As for the cause of our Gazell nostalgia; it was prompted by the memory of our trammel net experiment. A trammel net is a long net, over a hundred feet long and six feet deep, and we once placed this net in the tiny bay between the Minack side and the Gazell side. It was not, however, fixed to the Gazell side, but fixed to a buoy which was just short of the polar bear rock. Our intention, of course, was to become self-sufficient in fish. We were not successful. One night a gale blew up and blew the net away.

We perused the map; perused the Deeds. Neither of us had owned property before. The map was understandable; the Deeds mysterious.

'Sometimes I wonder, Jeannie,' I said, 'how we have done what we have done in our lives. Neither of us has a brain which is equipped to delve into detail.'

'I think we have common sense,' she said, 'and I think we both have intuition.'

My mind went back to a famous politician, Viscount Swinton. He was Secretary of State for Air before World War II and it was he who was the driving force behind the development of radar, and who organised the factory production of the Spitfire in time for the Battle of Britain. He took interest in my career, befriended me by recommending me to influential people, and I remember that he once said to me: 'Men may have great power, have great knowledge ... but if they do not possess the antennae of intuition they have nothing.'

'All right,' I said to Jeannie. 'Our common sense is telling us we are spending this money to buy this land because it is the only way we can ensure what we prize most ... tranquillity.'

'And our intuition,' added Jeannie, 'tells us that our whole life would have been destroyed if a stranger had bought it.'

'But aren't we being selfish?' I said. 'If a stranger had bought the land, he might have opened it up for the public. We want to keep it to ourselves.'

Jeannie paused, then she said: 'We'll share it with

dreamers and all those who find riches in solitude. These kind of people don't disturb tranquillity. It is the insensitive, bossy people who do that. People who are so frightened to look into themselves that they can never be alone but move around in groups, being aggressive about their so-called rights. These are the people we are seeking to avoid; not the dreamers. And anyhow they have the coastal path on our land.'

Later that morning, we put the Deeds and the map back into their large envelope, sealed it and posted it to our Falmouth solicitor. We now had to wait for the formal signing of the contract ... Michaelmas Day.

For it was on September 29th, Michaelmas Day, that Jeannie and I became landowners.

EIGHT

I took out the Condor before breakfast on Michaelmas Day.

The Condor is a formidable machine; a monster rotary cutter, and I career with it over the bulb meadows in late summer, cutting down the grass. Many of the meadows, however, are covered by high bracken, and then I plunge the machine through the bracken, pulverising it.

'Stay here,' I suggested to Jeannie, 'while I make the path. You can watch me through the bedroom window.'

The eighteen acres, except for the two fields, were mostly covered by bracken, jungle-high bracken, and my purpose was to cut a path through it so that, after breakfast, we could take a celebration walk.

'I was remembering the fire which swept through all that land,' said Jeannie, 'and it left everything a charred mess ... yet by the spring the bluebells were blooming again and we walked across to Carn Barges, Monty following us. Doesn't seem all that time ago.'

'Even then, we were wanting to own it.'

'Where are you going to cut the path?' Jeannie asked.

'I don't really know. I'll just have to find my way.'

'Make it a token celebration path. Don't try to do too much.'

'I'll manage.'

The trouble about driving the Condor blind through high bracken was that I would suddenly find myself crashing against a rock, or the blades, circulating at speed, would hit a collection of stones and would make a horrendous noise scraping against them. I had experienced this in the bulb meadows, and so I always preferred to choose a windy day when using the Condor rather than a still one. On a windy day my Condor work is not heard; on a still one the roar of the engine, the horrendous noise, echoes round the district.

This Michaelmas Day was a still one. As I went out from the cottage to go to the Condor, I heard, for instance, men talking in a fishing boat offshore, probably men in a crabber, and though I could not identify the words, there was this sound of conversation which proved how quiet was the morning.

Hence, I was aware when I started up the Condor that my activities were likely to be monitored. The roar of the engine, the horrendous noise … inevitably there could be distant people who might be wondering what Tangye was up to. No doubt I was being touchy. Why should I be concerned as to why anyone should wonder what I was up to?

The Condor beginning was simple. I drove it down the lane across Monty's Leap, my hands gripping the handle-bars, then up to the turn where stood the wooden gate on which Bill, a year or two back, had fixed the notice PRIVATE. I reached this gate, unlatched it, and drove the Condor into the field which Bill had explained was called the Clover field, and which was connected, on the side opposite the wooden gate, by the second of our fields known as the Clarence meadow. Perhaps I sound confusing. Clover field; Clarence meadow. Why should one be a field, the other a meadow? I do not know. In my experience it is a question of an irrational mood. Thus sometimes a field is a meadow; sometimes a meadow a field.

The Clover field was in two sections, in the sense that the middle of it had a depository of rocks and stone heaps and even a rusty, ancient iron plough and an equally ancient iron harrow, and so the link between the two sections was at each side. The bottom section was flat, edging the lane and the border stone hedge that was close to our small reservoir. It was this section where planning permission had been sought for an agricultural caravan and a septic tank.

The top section, the greater part of the field, resembled, when looked at from the gate, the gently rising side of a hill. It was this section which we could see most clearly from the cottage. It was in the right-hand corner of this section where we first saw the black cat who was to become Oliver. I was ruminating on the bridge at the time, when suddenly I saw a black spot moving along the grass at the top of the Clover field and, as I picked up my field-glasses, I called to Jeannie who was close by. The black spot became a black cat through the field-glasses and we proceeded to observe him become suddenly alert, poised in that well-known position of a cat about to pounce: a twitch of the tail, a slight backward and forward swaying motion, then a hesitancy, then the pounce ... and from our observation point we knew he had missed. He reacted to his embarrassment by obeying the late Paul Gallico's cat law: 'When in doubt, wash.'

We had observed other activities on the Clover field from the bridge. There was Whitepants, for instance. A light-coloured fox, who used to roam the Clover field looking for beetles, and he did not wait for evening to do so. We would see him in mid-morning, or in the afternoon, nosing in the grass and we would fear for him. He was such a sitting target for a gun.

There were cubs once in the Clover field. That right top corner, where we had seen Oliver, had a badger sett in the moorland on the other side of the hedge, and the badgers had made extensions of the sett under the hedge and into the Clover field. Often we had seen Bill fill in the entrances with rocks and earth because there was the danger that his tractor could be upset by lurching into one of the entrances. One spring, a pair of foxes took over one of the entrances and, during the early summer, we were to spend much time on the bridge watching their cubs, four of them, playing games around it. We feared, too, for them.

In our early years at Minack, the Clover field used to cause us much distress. Rabbits abounded in those days, and those were also the days when the gin trap was legal. We used to listen to the trapper tapping his hammer on a winter's afternoon and we would groan to each other, knowing that during the coming night we would be listening to the screams of the rabbits. Next morning, I would see, if I were standing on the bridge, the trapper walking round the Clover field gathering his harvest.

I saw my first pheasant in our district in the Clover field. A neighbouring farmer had introduced a number of young pheasants into the area, not to shoot, but for the fun of having them around. We did not know of this planned introduction until some while later, and so we had been astonished and intrigued by the sight of a splendid looking cock pheasant strutting in the Clover field, proclaiming his presence in a loud voice from time to time. Inevitably, Jeannie gave him a name and the name was Phineas. Then we became aware of his consort, a beige-brown bird, whose modest call sounded like a controlled chortle. Her name, Jeannie decided, was Phyllida.

These two by no means restricted their wanderings to the Clover field and its immediate neighbourhood, and we were soon to find them perambulating around Minack. I found Phineas one day resting under the apple tree, and he hurled epithets at me when I disturbed him. I was to learn also that he and Phyllida considered the inside of greenhouses irresistible.

They liked, for instance, to have a bath in them. I seldom witnessed such a bath in progress, but the evidence was there when I walked round . . . a dusty, round indentation of the soil. On the rare occasions when I caught one of them *in flagranza*, there was a wild cacophony and an hysterical banging of wings against glass, and then I would quickly retreat, leaving Phyllida or Phineas to find the way out at their leisure. However, once I gave Phineas a particular fright. Unknown to me, hidden by the foliage, he was having a bath between two rows of tomato plants ... when I turned on the water of the overhead spray lines.

Their survival seemed to me to be miraculous. They were such an easy target for our cliff foxes, and those people, wise in the way of pheasants, also told us that pheasants could not live in the far west because of the humid weather and they would surely die in the winter. Survival of the chicks seemed particularly miraculous, and I know of one occasion when a brood was drowned in a thunderstorm. I had seen them, a half dozen or more, following Phyllida along in the Clover field one summer evening; then came the thunderstorm and, next morning, I found them dead. However, Phyllida and Phineas have survived, so too some of their broods, and thus there is a scattering of Phyllidas and Phineases in our area and one of these, a Phineas, jerked fluttering and raucous into the sky as I drove the Condor up the Clover field on my way to make the celebration path.

I turned right at the top into a track which resembled a lane, in that both sides had a stone hedge, one bordering the Clover field, the other bordering one of the fields that the Falmouth Estate had bought. It was necessary, however, to search for the stone hedges because, over the years, elder, brambles and blackthorn had been burgeoning into the track. It was still wide enough for a tractor, but I realised the track would have to be regularly trimmed if it were to remain open. The blackthorn whetted my appetite, or rather my thirst. Sloes were clumped on the spiky branches and Jeannie was an expert in making sloe gin.

This track only ran the distance of the top of the Clover field, and then I came to an open stretch where in spring, I knew, bloomed gorse and bluebells, bracken in summer, and where badgers lived in one of the most historic setts in Cornwall. When the contract for the land was signed, one of the first things Jeannie said was, 'The badgers belong to us!'

And I replied, in sobering fashion, 'Maybe they do ... but Professor Zuckerman and the Ministry of Agriculture hold their destiny.'

The badger debate is never still, and those who refuse to accept the notion that badgers bring TB to cattle are accused of allowing their emotion to twist the facts. Personally, I think it is the other way round. Professor Zuckerman, who was to produce the anti-badger report, along with those who supported him, were so anxious to *prove* their case that they allowed the facts to tally with *their* emotions.

Individual badgers contract TB. That is a fact. But no more than flimsy evidence has been produced to prove that badgers in the wild infect cattle. As in all tricky situations, people like to find a scapegoat and especially, as in the badger case, those farmers who find they have an unhealthy herd. This is understandable, but it is bad luck on the badgers. Strange, I find, that over the centuries, for some unexplained reason, badgers have earned the hatred of sections of country people (the word badgering comes from such a hatred).

Anyone living in the country can suggest far more likely scapegoats; old farm buildings, for instance, which housed cattle decades ago when TB really was the scourge of cattle and which, in their dark corners, could have retained infection, just as seeds of the field can remain dormant for years. Bad husbandry could be another scapegoat, or overstocking of cattle, or migrating birds. Anyone who has seen a giant flock of starlings descend on a field can imagine what diseases they could have brought with them from afar.

Badgers, however, also have friends among farmers. I know of one farmer who felt so strongly when Ministry officials began trapping badgers on the next-door farm that he sneaked over the hedge at night and set the traps off. His family had farmed the same land for a hundred years and his cattle had never been infected by TB. Indeed, the badgers to him are like pets. They even come to the milking parlour at milking time and he pours them a bowl of milk.

Gassing is the main method used by the Ministry to eliminate badgers, and of course this means a wholesale slaughter in the sett concerned. Evidence is first collected from badger droppings (badgers are so hygienically fastidious that they mark out a lavatory patch at a distance from their sett), and if the test in any single instance is positive, the order goes out to gas the sett. It is an order reminiscent of the Nazi gas chambers.

However, to be fair, Ministry officials are conscientious in their search for TB evidence. They do not act unless cattle TB is reported in the area, and then the setts within a certain radius come under scrutiny. Nonetheless, the fact remains that the analysis of TB in a badger does not prove that the badger has infected the cattle. This is the weakness of Professor Zuckerman's *Report on Badgers, Cattle and Tuberculosis*. No factual evidence is produced to show that badgers in the wild have anything to do with TB in cattle.

Indeed there is evidence available which proves the contrary. A farmer friend of mine found a dead badger on his land and notified the Ministry of Agriculture. On examination, TB was identified in the badger and, since another farm not far away had suffered a reactor in its herd (a reactor is a cow who has reacted to a TB test and is, therefore, probably infected), an examination was made of a large badger sett in the area. Tests of droppings showed evidence of TB and so the sett was gassed.

However, what was significant in this case was that the cattle which grazed the land around where the sett was situated and had done so for years had never been infected by TB. Badgers all around and no TB. Someone asked the official in charge of the sett-gassing how he explained this. He could not.

TB in cattle is fortunately in any case a rarity, and it certainly does not merit the traditional persecution of the badger. There is a far more sinister disease for Professor Zuckerman to investigate, and that is brucellosis. Drinkers of milk from a cow infected with brucellosis, milk which has not been boiled, may develop a form of dizziness which may persist for a few days, then disappear, then develop again later. Recently there was a scare of widespread brucellosis amongst the wandering cattle of Dartmoor.

I drove the Condor on past the sett, thinking of Professor Zuckerman and the power he held over the future of badgers everywhere, and I thought, a nervous thought, as to what Jeannie would do if ever a Zuckerman acolyte declared that *her* badgers had to be gassed. Her father was an officer in the London Scottish, until he was himself gassed during the First World War; and when he died, he left her his sword, which she keeps in a cupboard. This sword is treated by Jeannie like a weapon which authorities keep back in reserve for extreme emergencies. I have heard her, for instance, say that she would pierce any intruder with it should they come . . . and I then quietly explain to her that, although she might be morally right in defending her home, the law would put her in jail for doing so. The sword has also been mentioned by her in connection with the defence of the badgers. I trust there never will be a need to restrain her.

I reached the first dense thicket of bracken after passing the sett, and the bracken was head high, and I was driving the Condor blind. The experience, as I have said, was not new to me. Every year, on the Minack daffodil fields, I swear I will proceed to cut them down before the bracken, or the grass, have grown to maturity. In dry years it does not matter because the growth is comparatively small . . . but in wet years the bracken and the grass go beserk, and this means that the Condor is harder to handle.

When the bracken and any other undergrowth is dense, I lean on the handlebars of the Condor so that the blades, though adjusted to their highest level, still have a little more height. I have to do this because the blades would otherwise become clogged with what they are cutting. I thus lean on the handlebars, the engine roaring, finding myself being buffeted by the various directions the terrain leads the Condor, and I find myself thinking that any athlete, boxer, footballer or long-distance runner could not adopt a better training system than following the activity of a daffodil grower in late summer, preparing for the daffodil harvest of spring.

In the many small daffodil meadows that tumble down towards the sea, the Condor, of course, is too big to use, and then the Japanese Brush Cutter, an equally punishing machine, takes its place. The Brush Cutter, seven feet long, has a circular blade driven by a small engine, and it is held by a harness slung across my shoulders. I take the machine down to the bottom of the cliff and make my way upwards, from meadow to meadow. This is another exercise suitable for an athlete in training. I sway the revolving circular blade from side to side in the manner of the old-fashioned scythe, cutting the bracken and the undergrowth, and peeling the hedges of brambles. Without such machines as the Condor and the Brush Cutter, I would not be able to work the land on my own.

I work these machines, for the most part, anonymously. I do not like to be watched. I feel embarrassed if someone is staring at me when one of the machines is lunging me this way or that. Hence, if I have to work one of the meadows in the vicinity of the coastal path, I choose a time to do so when I do not expect anyone to be about.

It so happens that I also make it my business to keep the

115

coastal path across Minack land open, and this entails me using the Condor along it from time to time. I do this voluntarily because it helps to make the way easy for walkers, and I was performing my task one evening this summer when I went back in time to when servants were plentiful. For two elderly, tweedy ladies came down the path towards me and, as the path was narrow, I thought it wise to stop the engine while they passed. As they did so, one of them said in patronising fashion:

'Well done, my man. You're doing a most useful job.'

Metaphorically, I touched my cap.

I did not go far, bearing in mind what Jeannie had said, in making the celebration path. I was driving the Condor blind, but this was not as blind as I make it appear. For I knew there was a track where I was making the path, just as I knew there were other tracks, now hidden by bracken and undergrowth, on the rest of the eighteen acres. It was just a question of finding them; just as it was a question of finding the track for the celebration path. I was making good progress when I was suddenly faced by a hump of granite rock and, when I swerved to avoid it, the blades of the Condor crashed into another hazard, a collection of dislodged hedge stones and, for a moment, until I switched off the engine, there was the horrendous clatter of the blades against the stones. At this point, therefore, I decided the celebration path had been completed. There would be time enough to continue the path round the land and, in due course, make other paths.

So I returned to the cottage, and to breakfast.

'Do you think,' said Jeannie, 'that everyone feels as we now feel when, for the first time, they walk on land they own?'

'I don't suppose property developers do,' I said. 'They just think what a good deal they've done and the money they can make out of it.'

'Anyhow,' said Jeannie, 'we have worked for this moment. The land hasn't dropped into our laps. It has been a long journey. Let's go and walk the celebration path.'

Breakfast was over; I was sitting in the porch and I heard the fluting sound of curlews flying west over the cottage, and then there was a clatter on the glass roof of the porch. I looked up and saw the webbed feet of Philip the gull. His presence on the glass roof sometimes annoyed me. The porch became very hot when the sun chose to shine, and so I would painstakingly shade the outside glass with a special white mixture and then, as the days went by, I would have to endure the sight of Philip strutting on the glass, continuously scratching the white shading until little was left of it, and Jeannie would then begin gently to urge me that the time had come for me to get up on the ladder and shade it again.

'Better feed Philip before we go,' I said in the tone of voice of someone who has to pay blackmail money, 'and Ron is up there too.'

Ron was the rook who lived in Lamorna Valley but, for three years or so, he had been feeding with us. He once had a wife called Eth, but she died, and ever since he has been daily coming to us on his own.

'And another thing,' I said, 'there are plenty of blackberries up there on the path. While you feed the birds, I'll fetch a couple of packs.'

The packs I referred to were a relic of a moment in our Cornish life when we believed we were about to make a fortune. We were among the first to think of selling bulbs in polythene packs. We had a pack of a very pretty design, and we were so ebulliently hopeful that we ordered twenty-five thousand of them. We still have twenty-four thousand left. Since they have air-holes in them we cannot use them as freezer packs, and thus their only purpose today is for blackberry picking and for sloe picking. We use perhaps twenty a year.

As we left, Fred and Merlin were staring down at us from the field above the cottage. Their turn would come. Later we would introduce them to their new green world.

Then, as we walked down towards Monty's Leap, I asked

Jeannie where Ambrose might be, and she replied that he disappeared after I had set out to create the celebration path and there had been no sign of him since.

A wood-pigeon made a noisy exit from an elm tree close to Monty's Leap.

'They're going,' I said. 'The elm trees. I've counted ten of them with the disease.'

We were both, I believe, a little self-conscious. This was one of the moments in life when endeavour was having its reward, and I think there was a nervousness, a fear, that we might not measure up to the enormity of the moment. People who have striven in any sphere have such doubts when achievement is realised. It is this great chasm which separates those who struggle for a reward, and those who expect rewards as a right. The strugglers can hardly believe their achievement is true. The others rile against such achievement coming to pass.

'What are we going to call this land,' said Jeannie. 'We must have a name for it.'

'That is your province, isn't it?'

A gentle joke.

'Well, I know what I would like to call it.'

'And what's that?'

'I think it ought to be called Oliver land ... after all, we saw him there first and, if it hadn't been for him, your books wouldn't be in America and Japan and France and Germany ... and there wouldn't have been an Ambrose.'

'I agree with that. Some people might call it sentimental.'

'Oh,' said Jeannie, 'I am so fed up with these clever people who knock the word sentimental. What have they got to offer in its place? Their clever clap-trap is so empty of anything worthwhile. All they do is to try to make an effect.'

'Jeannie, darling,' I said, laughing at her. 'We're on a celebration walk and it is a quiet morning on a Cornish cliff.'

'I'm just fed up with the fakes,' said Jeannie.

'We had, by now, reached the gate that opened into the

Clover field and I had untied the string which connected the gate to the gatepost when, behind me, came the sound of a miniature yap and this was followed by rapturous noises from Jeannie. Ambrose.

'*What* are you doing here?' asked Jeannie, bending down. '*Where* have you been?'

I shuffled by the gate. This was Jeannie in the full flight of cat language, and I had planned a quiet walk on the celebration path. Ambrose was going to hold us up. Ambrose was going to spoil the occasion.

'Leave him,' I said irritably. 'I want to show you what I've done. Leave the cat alone.'

'Leave the cat alone? What did I hear you say?'

'This is special ... I don't want to miss it. The moment, I mean.'

Jeannie, sensing that my dormant anti-cat attitude was rising to the surface, responded.

'He doesn't want you,' she said, speaking down to Ambrose. 'You'll have to stay here.'

But he did not stay there.

He followed us. I had never known him follow us so far from the cottage. He even stopped half-way up the Clover field and made his mark, proclaiming to every other wandering cat that they were on Ambrose territory.

He followed us to the right, towards the badger sett. He was trotting behind us confidently. There was no doubtful miaow. He sniffed at a badger hole, then another, and my mind went back to an occasion when Lama went down a badger hole, and we spent hours and hours persuading her to come out.

Ambrose passed the badger sett.

Then we were walking the true celebration path, the path where the Condor had pulverised the bracken, until we came to a sudden stop at the hump of granite rock which had been hidden in the head-high bracken.

Ambrose, too, came to a stop at the rock.

He jumped up on it and, without hesitation, began to purr.

NINE

We sat on the rock for a while, feet dangling, Ambrose between us, purring. A granite slab of rock, aeons old.

'An Everest moment,' said Jeannie.

Jeannie's definition of an Everest moment is when a long-awaited occasion totally measures up to expectation.

'Do you know what I'm going to call this rock?' went on Jeannie.

Another name for her to invent.

'What is it to be?' I asked.

'The Ambrose Rock.'

'An Everest moment . . . the Ambrose Rock. Yes, I see the connection.'

'I'll never for the rest of my life forget this moment,' Jeannie said, 'and I'll come and touch the Ambrose Rock and relive it.'

'You're a romantic.'

'You know I am . . . like you.'

On either side of the rock, and behind us, was a forest of grey-green bracken, soon to be winter brown. It had lost its summer strength and was keeling over, forming into a wave of dense mats. In front of us was a scrub of odd-shaped gorse waiting to brighten winter with its yellow blooms, the gnarled branches covered by a glove of bearded lichen, the lichen which only grows in the purest air.

Beyond the gorse, the sun was rising above the Lizard, shining on the vast expanse of Mount's Bay, and to our left, a few miles off Mousehole, was a cluster of hand-line mackerel boats, and then nearer to the shore, sailing west towards Gwennap Head and Land's End, we suddenly saw a lifeboat, the crew on deck in their bright orange oilskins.

'The Sennen lifeboat,' I said, having heard on the local news bulletin that she had taken an injured seaman to Newlyn.

The Sennen lifeboat crew have a special place in Cornwall's sea history, for the lifeboat station is situated in Sennen Cove on a site which, to the amateur, appears to be specially dangerous. For, when the lifeboat dives down the ramp and into the sea, rocks abound in the area; and one marvels how on a dark stormy night, seamanship can avoid such rocks. The crews of the Sennen lifeboat have saved many lives, and brought comfort to many seamen who were foundering in the wild Land's End seas.

Maurice Hutchens is today the coxswain of the lifeboat, and we knew him first when he was an apprentice carpenter to the Thomas family of St Buryan; father called Ashley, son called Harold, craftsmen both, whose first job in helping us to make Minack habitable was to put a roof to the cottage. During this period, I said to Maurice that we specially enjoyed mullet, and Sennen Cove is periodically the scene of a great concourse of mullet entering the bay. A shout goes up through the village, and every Cove-er present hastens to help net the invasion.

On one such occasion, when Maurice was an apprentice, he

bicycled from Sennen Cove to Minack ... with a mullet as a gift.

There was another occasion, after a mullet invasion had been reported on the local news, that a large group of Cornishmen from a distant part of Cornwall hastened to Sennen Cove in vans and motor cars to take part in the catch of the mullet invasion, the invasion which Sennen Cove-ers had cherished as their special reserve for so long. The intruders, as they came down the steep hill, were threatened with a barrage of local missiles and shouting men and women telling them to go away. It was as if a tribe were having to repel the attack of another tribe. Of course, the Cove-ers were victorious and the rival tribe never dared try to catch a Sennen Cove mullet again.

We could see the cottage to our right as we sat on the rock, nestling squat among the trees on the other side of the valley. Strange to see it from this view. Strange to see the land which, over the years, we had worked, had been the inspiration of our hopes, had been a part of our failures and successes, outlined there on the other side of the valley ... and being so *small* in area.

We could not see it all, of course. There was the curving line of the top of the valley, a silhouette of a curve, which traced downwards to the sea, and to the cliff meadows which were out of sight from where we sat on the rock. Nor could we see the greenhouses, and the field above where grew the white narcissi which followed the yellows. Nor could we see the wood meadow which we knew first as a bog; before draining it with earthenware pipes, and planting first Golden Harvest, which failed; then Joseph McLeod, which have blossomed. I was digging the ditches for the earthenware pipes when Alan Whicker and his TV unit came to interview us. My picture on the screen showed me with a long handle shovel digging a ditch ... after Alan Whicker had taken Jeannie aside and, in order to bring spark to the programme, an understandable professional necessity, had asked her:

'What do you quarrel about?'

We could see, however, from where we sat, the special areas of our early endeavours, the areas where the main sources of income had been derived. There was the land, divided in meadows, on either side of the coastal path where some of our Obvallaris grew; some of our Actaea and King Alfred and California, and the lovely daffodil with the ugly name of Sulphur. Over the years, these meadows had been so important to us, had caused us to worry as to when the blooms should be picked, caused us to bemoan the price they received in the market; but on occasions to rejoice ... these meadows had been a vital ingredient of our life; the harvest, the dying down of the leaves and the summer growth of weeds, the autumn cutting down, the December sight of the first daffodil green spike, and the harvest again. Our survival depended upon them and the other land which we could not see as we sat on the rock, but it all seemed so *small*.

'We now have the space to expand,' I said to Jeannie. 'We could open up the bracken-covered meadows; have five tons of bulbs in the Clover field ...'

She broke into laughter.

'I thought the whole idea was to leave everything as it is.'

'I feel differently now that we actually own the land.'

'I don't,' said Jeannie. 'You have enough to do as it is ... and just think of the labour costs!'

'I'm tempted. I'm going to see what I can work out. Anyhow, Bill had daffodils in some of the meadows. I'll have to find them and open them up.'

'I prefer the idea of keeping it as a Nature Reserve,' Jeannie said; and, at that moment, Ambrose jumped down from the rock.

'It would be soothing to have a Nature Reserve. I don't think I could stand the anxieties of expansion.'

'Anyhow, we'll have to make up our minds.'

Ambrose played the stop and run game as we walked back to the cottage, along the path, down the slope of the Clover field, then up the lane. He would scamper ahead, wait until I had caught up with him and appear to want me to pick him up; but when I stooped to do so, he would race away again ... a split second escape from my reach.

We arrived back at the cottage and Jeannie led Ambrose away or, more accurately, Ambrose followed Jeannie ... to a saucer of fish. We wanted him out of the way when we introduced the donkeys to their new world. So, with Ambrose engrossed in his fish, we went up to the gate of the donkey field above the cottage where the donkeys were waiting.

Maddeningly, they performed their bottom act. It had happened often before. The donkeys would be demanding our attention, demanding to be changed from one field to another and yet, when we reached them, they would turn their bottoms upon us. It happened on this occasion. We picked up their halters, approached them as their heads were leaning over the gate ... and with the measured movement of elephants they walked away from us.

'This is a great occasion!' I called out. 'Fred! Merlin! We're wanting to introduce you to a great new world. Acres to wander about it; a paradise of new grasses and brambles ... Come on, Fred!'

They were displaying their power. They were attempting to show that obedience was not a corollary to bossmanship. Persuade us to do what you want us to do; don't order us.

Having made their gesture, they became amenable. We lassooed them with their halters, took them through the gate, down the steep path past the cottage, Fred on the way taking a swipe at the *escallonia*, and then on we went up the lane to the gate of the Clover field.

We opened the gate and took off the halters, and away went the donkeys. They behaved as if they were in a Calgary stampede. Back legs flying, heads down, turning in tight circles, then racing away up the Clover field, and around by the corner where we first saw Oliver, then along the top of the field and down towards us, and veering away when they saw us, as if they were revelling in a mad rush of happiness, but which might have been smothered by some action on our part. What Jeannie and I were watching was an example of natural freedom. We all want to obtain it, this freedom which is not created by laws, but by the joyousness of suddenly finding oneself freed from inhibitions and secret fears and the raging stresses of today. The donkeys were, at this moment, a manifestation of the freedom that the human race seeks. They were in a new world. There was nothing foreseeable at this moment which would ever spoil it. It was fresh. There would never be an end. This was an Everest moment for the donkeys.

The little red van of the postman came down the lane soon after we had returned to the cottage and, among the letters I opened as I sat on the sofa, was one from a friend who had been a colleague of mine in MI5. My friend in his letter indignantly condemned a smear campaign that was being conducted against my one-time chief in MI5, the late Captain Guy Liddell, a campaign which alleged that he had been a KGB agent, and that it was he who had tipped off Guy Burgess and Donald Maclean in 1951, enabling them to escape to the Soviet Union. The letter shed away the happy moments of the morning, and my mind went back to the London days before we came to Cornwall.

Guy Liddell had been for a long time a friend of my father, and I first met him before World World Two when he and his wife lived in a magnificent Lutyens house, now pulled down, in Chelsea. I was a reporter on a Sunday newspaper at the time, very impecunious, and Guy and his wife used to lend me an Austin Seven to take my girl friends around. One such girl, though only as an acquaintance did she remain, was a beautiful, sloe-eyed American movie actress called Sylvia Sydney. I had fallen in love with her as I sat in the Empire Cinema, Leicester Square, watching her in a movie called *Street Scene*, and when one day she came to London to act in a film, I persuaded my editor to send me to interview her. At the end of the interview, I asked if she would have dinner with me that evening. To my surprise, she said she would. I hurriedly contacted Guy Liddell, who once again agreed to loan me the Austin Seven and, in due course, I arrived outside Claridge's where she was staying, and took her off to the Quo Vadis restaurant in Soho. I had explained to her that I would show her London and, after dinner, we roamed London in the Austin, until we ended up on the Embankment opposite Battersea Power Station. It was floodlit. It was magnificent. The evening, alas, had not been magnificent. I had been so amazed to be in the presence of a movie star with whom I had fallen in love from a seat in the Empire Cinema, that I had been tongue-tied.

I lost touch with Guy Liddell when I went away from London for a year, travelling round the world. War broke out soon after I returned and I enlisted in the Duke of Cornwall's Light Infantry. I had been in the ranks for three months, when I was summoned for an interview at the War Office and, shortly afterwards, I was given a commission. In those wonderland days of the Phoney War period, the War Office had found just the man they had been looking for to take charge of the Order of Battle of the Chinese Armies. I was the man. I had the qualifications. I had had a quick peep at China. I had visited Manchuria. I had travelled on the Trans-Siberian Express. Hence, I became ensconced in the War Office with a large map, upon which I pinned little flags as to where the divisions of the Chinese Armies were garrisoned and, with the meagre information available, made out reports on the communications in China ... for instance.

'Chunking-Kweiyang: At Wukiang there is invariably a bad hold up owing to lack of ferryboats.'

This feeble war effort on my part was acceptable during the Phoney War. But one night I was night-duty officer at the War Office, the night of May 9th/10th, 1940, when I was awakened on my iron bedstead by a telephone call from the Military Attaché in Brussels.

'The balloon is up,' he cried. 'The German Army half an hour ago began crossing the Belgian frontier.'

I realised that I was a pivot in a moment of history and that not a second was to be lost. I seized another telephone and rang, according to standard instructions, the Deputy Chief of Staff of the British Army. 'Good show,' he said, after hearing my news. 'Now we can get moving.'

I began to observe, as I continued to pin my flags on my Chinese map, the cosy attitudes of those in charge on the Home Front. While the British Army in France was fighting its rearguard action to Dunkirk, the mandarins of Whitehall were content to write memos to one another. In my favoured position of Officer in Charge of the Chinese Armies, I was on the special list to be supplied with copies of many of these communications. As the German paratroops dropped from the skies, as the Panzer divisions swept forward, as the Fifth Column caused chaos among the Belgian, Dutch and French populations, I developed a despair at the languid, unimaginative way the home hierarchy were approaching the situation. Our troops were fighting and dying, but at home the hierarchy were dealing out verbal sleeping pills.

The ultimate complacency seemed to be reached when I read a memo summarising a Chiefs of Staff's meeting in the third week of May. The Chiefs of Staff instructed the secretary to draft for their approval a report to the War Cabinet, drawing their attention to the need for a higher state of readiness in the United Kingdom, and to the danger of a seaborne raid on a large scale by fast motor boats, which the Navy would have difficulty in intercepting, and accompanied by airborne raids inland.

Europe disintegrating, and here was the snail-pace response of the Chiefs of Staff.

Meanwhile, my newspaper mind had had an idea, and this I decided to outline in a letter to the legendary head of MI6, Colonel Menzies. I had never met him, but he too was a friend of my father. Here are the main points of the letter, dated May 20th, 1940:

'I put this idea direct to you because I feel the urgency of the situation absolves me from putting it forward through the "usual channels". This is the idea:

1. It is based on the assumption of the invasion of Britain by Germany.
2. In this event, agents no doubt will have to be organised to operate behind their lines.
3. I suggest that the basis of such an organisation should be set up immediately in the following way:

(a) In each area where airborne troops can be landed, someone should be appointed who knows the locality and local inhabitants intimately.
(b) Under him should be locals who up to the present probably have little knowledge of military affairs.
(c) These should be instructed as soon as possible regarding what constitutes information of military value.
(d) Finally the question of the sending out of the information should be considered - the establishment of radio transmitting sets, etc.'

Four days later I had a reply. Once again a snail pace reaction.

'I always like new ideas and, for that reason, your letter of the 20th was welcome. I do not say what you suggest is practical, but it will receive consideration when plans are evolved.'

A couple of weeks later, however, there was a curious sequel to this correspondence. My father told me he was coming up from his home in Cornwall and that he would be at his London Club on a certain evening. I went along there to see him and found him in the leather-chaired library, talking to a well groomed, distinguished-looking civilian.

'This is Colonel Menzies,' said my father, introducing me. An instinct stopped me from referring to the correspondence; nor did Colonel Menzies refer to it. Indeed, within a few minutes, he had said goodbye and left. My father was smiling.

'I've got a job!' said my father, who, like many of his generation, did not want to feel too old for the war. 'A worthwhile job which I can do well ... They're organising a secret service behind the lines should the Germans invade, and I am to be in charge of the South West.'

To this day, I find it strange that Colonel Menzies never referred to the contents of my letter. I never met him again.

In August 1940, I was transferred to MI5. I had a spell in Newcastle, where I was assistant to Kenneth Younger, later to become Minister of State for Foreign Affairs in the Labour government after the war, and then I was brought back to London. Guy Liddell had given the order for me to do so. I had not seen him since the days of my borrowing the Austin Seven, but now he was head of B division of MI5, and he had a special assignment for me.

It had been decided that it was wrong to keep the work of the various MI5 Sections isolated from each other, and so it had been proposed that a news-sheet should be periodically produced outlining the current work of each Section. It was my task to go round each Section asking them to write up their various activities, and it was understandable that the heads of these Sections were reluctant to do so. Nonetheless, the information I collected was of great interest. Since Philby and Anthony Blunt were on the circulation list, and the Soviet Union was still not at war with Germany, it must have been of still greater interest to them.

At first, I produced my news-sheet from a cell in Wormwood Scrubs, which MI5 had taken over, and then the organisation was evacuated to Blenheim Palace, home of the Dukes of Marlborough, and I continued my work from there. This did not last for long, because the scope of my work had been enlarged and I returned to London and was given a flat in Dolphin Square where I could work independently of the main MI5 organisation. Guy Liddell, at all times, was the man who superintended this freedom, although it was Viscount Swinton, then chairman of the Security Executive, who proposed that I should also be attached for special duties with the Secretary of the Cabinet. I then proceeded to meet the Secretary of the Cabinet, Sir Edward Bridges, every Monday throughout the year until the end of the war.

I also saw the heads of MI5 Departments on Monday every week, and gave them a summary of the information, factual, gossip, rumour and suspicions, that had been gathered by my Section during the previous seven days; and much of this was also used in various interpretations by the Doublecross Section, which achieved the fabulous success of deceiving the German High Command.

Philby, because he was not a member of MI5, though working so closely with it, never attended my Monday meetings; nor did Blunt. Indeed my personal dealings with Philby were rare. On one occasion, he asked me to recruit a suitable person to act as an agent in Lisbon on his Section's behalf, and I received his thanks after I had arranged this. Philby, presumably, then informed his KGB masters of the man's name.

Another occasion concerned a German diplomat, who had defected to the British and who, in order to prove that he was a genuine defector, had brought with him a list of prominent Germans who were opposed to Hitler. During his interrogation, however, it became clear that the prominent Germans involved were in even greater opposition to the prospect of the Soviet army taking over Germany, and the diplomat had believed that this information would be of vital interest to the Western Allies; perhaps encourage the Western Allies to institute early peace negotiations with the prominent Germans on the list. The diplomat stayed in our house at Mortlake, and Jeannie and I were witness to the tortured struggle suffered by a man who has defected because he believes he is helping his countrymen by doing so.

British Intelligence, in the guise of Philby, made note of

the names, and I was given the task of soothing the diplomat from his role of a defector into the mundane, frustrating role of a defector who had to find a job. At least, he believed his mission had been successfully completed. He was not to know that he had misread the political situation and that the Western Allies had no intention of negotiating a separate peace. Philby, however, was interested in his mission. My tortured diplomat friend had supplied him with all the names the KGB required.

There are sections of the media and of the academic world which periodically try to turn Philby into a folk hero. This attitude enrages me. Few men in history have crept into old age with so much blood on their hands.

I cannot say, even in retrospect, that Blunt had the aura of a Soviet spy. Philby, I can say in retrospect, had such an aura. I remember facing him, for the first time, over his desk in his office in Ryder Street off St James's, and sensing a curious look in his eyes as if he were sizing me up. The experience chilled me and, later that day, when I saw Jeannie, I told her about it. Blunt never had that chilling effect on me.

Blunt, with whom I first made contact at the bar which was improvised in the dining room of Blenheim Palace, seemed to me to behave like an excitable undergraduate. Very tall, usually in the uniform of a captain in the Intelligence Corps, and I specially remember how the bottom part of the jacket of his uniform was always flapping against him as he rushed around. My memory of him is that he was always rushing. He rushed out his conversation, brimful with academic theories; he rushed across the quadrangle in front of the Palace and, when later MI5 moved to a building in St James's Street, London, I remember him rushing down the corridors.

I was no friend of his. He belonged to a clique in MI5, and I have never, from schooldays onwards, been accepted as a suitable member of a clique. As a schoolboy this worried me because, in the popularity stakes, it seemed of importance to be a member of a clique but, as I grew older, I was to find it a blessing to be considered the odd man out. One can, as a result, keep one's personal freedom. One never has to go with the herd.

I might not have been a friend of Blunt, but he was frequently in professional touch with me. I might, one morning, step aside as he swept down a corridor with two or three members of his clique, reminding me of the arrogance of school prefects, and an hour later he could be on the telephone to me, asking a question that only my Section could answer.

I never considered the questions he asked of me were of particular significance, though they covered a wide range of topics and personalities. I do remember one report I sent to him concerning Guy Burgess, whom I knew was a close friend of Blunt. I told Blunt that I had heard that Burgess had been asking very pertinent questions of a foreign diplomat at a dinner party, and that the diplomat had jumped to the conclusion that Burgess was asking the questions on behalf of the British Secret Service. I suggested to Blunt that Burgess should be warned to be more discreet in the future. The diplomat's conjecture was wrong, of course, and I too was wrong. I knew that Burgess did special work for Blunt . . . but I did not know that the work was on behalf of the KGB.

The smear campaign against Guy Liddell began after Blunt had been exposed, twenty years after Guy had died. So easy to smear the reputations of those who are dead. Many biographers earn a living by doing so. In Guy Liddell's case, the smear campaign was orchestrated by a deathbed interview which Dr Goronwy Rees, a one-time friend of Burgess and Blunt, gave to Andrew Boyle, author of *The Climate of Treason*. Dr Rees inferred that Guy Liddell was the man who had tipped off Burgess and Maclean to flee the country because Maclean was about to be interrogated. Sometimes I have wondered whether the authorities of the day decided to let them flee the country so the government could escape the political embarrassment, especially American reaction, that an Old Bailey trial would have involved.

Dr Goronwy Rees, however, in starting the smear campaign, argued that circumstantial evidence suggested that Guy Liddell was a long-term Soviet agent, and had tipped off Burgess within a short time of the decision to interrogate Maclean having been made. Others joined in to attack Guy Liddell, rivals of the past who were wishing to gain revenge. However, Guy Liddell, such an amiable man, one of the finest chamber orchestra cellists in the country, a man who was always ready to listen to any of his staff; a man who, every night after the day's work was over, dictated a diary describing every aspect of the day's events ... proved to have powerful friends.

Sir Dick White, head of MI5 from 1953-56, head of MI6 from 1956-69, co-ordinator of intelligence and security in the Cabinet Office from 1970-73, indignantly wrote to *The Times* and to Andrew Boyle, defending Guy Liddell's reputation. Another indignant friend, who made public his view, was the legendary Mr Skardon, ace interrogator of spies, who had worked closely with Guy Liddell over the years.

Why then did Dr Goronwy Rees, on his deathbed, make such accusations? The answer may lie in the fact that he was dying in the shadow of having been suspected of being a Soviet agent himself. He confessed, in his last interview with Andrew Boyle, that he had known both Burgess and Blunt had been Soviet agents since he first became a friend of Burgess in 1936. Yet Rees had not told anyone. He observed Blunt climbing in his career, knew he had joined MI5, then become Keeper of the Queen's Pictures. He watched Burgess weave his charm into influential circles, saw him appointed to the Washington Embassy, and admired him when he became personal assistant to Hector McNeil, Minister of State at the Foreign Office.

Yet he did not reveal his knowledge to any member of the British Security Services; he kept his secret about Burgess and

Blunt to himself for over forty years. Why?

Perhaps it was his conscience that was being reflected in his deathbed interview. Or was it possible, as a last gesture, that he was trailing a false scent? And that, by accusing Guy Liddell, he believed he was leading the security services away from someone else? A public figure, perhaps, who was still alive?

As far as contemporary criticism of MI5 is concerned, one has to bear in mind the climate of opinion during the war and immediately afterwards. While the Soviet Union was an ally, numerous prominent people, the fringe spies, were saying openly that the Western Allies were not being frank enough with the Soviet Union; and so, when they passed information which reached the KGB, their behaviour could be viewed in no worse a light than a Cabinet leak.

The professional spies, of course, come into another category, but their successes were also greatly helped by the climate of opinion of the time. In *The Way To Minack*, I wrote:

'I believe that one of the reasons for the MI5 failure after the war was due to over-sensitiveness. There was a strong undercurrent of prejudice against MI5 in many prominent circles, and it showed itself in a curious way. People would proclaim that they were being persecuted by MI5, and gained prestige by so proclaiming: "My telephone is being tapped ...", "My letters are being opened ...", "I am being followed." This persecution mania was probably fanned by Soviet agents as a part of a nerve war against MI5, and it was a campaign which had a measure of success. My salient impression of MI5 had always been that it judged a person brought to their notice objectively ... but this campaign influenced MI5 to be too objective. MI5 wanted at all cost to avoid the stigma of being called the British version of the Soviet secret police. MI5 was, therefore, scared into being too cautious.'

Thus, when the media and politicians of today pursue their spy investigations, they should bear in mind the climate of opinion that existed, and also bear in mind that their predecessors in the media and in politics helped, by their attacks on MI5, to make the life of a Soviet spy so much safer.

There is one aspect, however, of the whole affair which intrigues me. Who has leaked the information, true or false, about these long-ago spies who are now of no use to the KGB, except for propaganda purposes? A permanent policy of the KGB is to denigrate the Establishment of every Western nation.

All this is another world to our life at Minack, and I was brought back to reality by a knock at the door and the appearance of a young woman.

'I'm married now,' she said, 'but I was a Jelbert ... Jean Jelbert. I live in Warwick. My father worked for Tom Laity until he left Cornwall to live in the Midlands.'

I remembered her father. I used to have a pointless joke with him during the early potato season. Tom Laity's meadows dovetailed with ours, and I used to make this pointless joke whenever we were all tired and hot after digging up the new potatoes with our shovels.

'Never mind,' I would say, voicing my pointless joke, 'thundery rain will be coming soon.'

For some reason 'thundery rain' always raised a wry smile from Jelbert. It was an 'in' joke of the Cornish potato season.

'I used to come here as a child,' said the young woman, 'and I had such happy times that I have treasured them as if they serve as an anchor in my life.'

There have been others who have returned to Minack. An old woman came once, and told us that as a child before the First World War she used to dance barefooted with her friends around Minack, pretending it was a fairy cottage.

Then there were the two young men I saw one summer's day, standing by the barn and staring at the cottage. When I went out and talked to them, they told me they had spent a year at Minack during the war years when they were children. Their father was a Captain in the Royal Navy, and they and their mother were living in a farm cottage nearby when, one day, the farmer turned them out. Their mother then led them across the fields, carrying their possessions, and made a home in empty Minack. An earth floor, a leaking roof, a barrel to catch the rainwater. For the two boys and their mother, however, it was heaven.

'We grew violets,' one of them said to me, 'in a little three-cornered meadow over there,' he was pointing towards the bridge, 'and sometimes we would stand there, watching the convoys crossing Mount's Bay towards the Lizard.'

Since that day of the young men's visit, I have often stood in that three-cornered meadow, thinking of those violets, and the children who picked them, and the mother staring out to sea.

'I used to come here to visit two old ladies, sisters,' went on the young woman. 'Our home then was at Moorcroft on the way to St Buryan, and I would walk the two or three miles, always knowing that I would have a wonderful welcome at the end of my walk. They were very funny, these two old ladies. For some reason they never had a kettle. They used to fill a large saucepan with rainwater from the waterbutt, and let it simmer on the stove. It always was a long wait for a cup of tea.

'Then there were the mice! They treated mice as other people treat pets. I used to sit there and see a mouse come scurrying across the floor and run across the shoe of one of the old ladies, and she never took any notice at all!'

We also had suffered Minack mice experience. Monty, Lama, Oliver, Ambrose, all had made their mice contributions to the cottage from time to time. If left as a present on the carpet, it was my job quickly to remove them. If alive, we would ask for the cooperation of the donor, who seldom felt in the mood to oblige. One live mouse, an Ambrose donation, caused a major household disturbance. Night after night came the sound of scratching from the kitchen. I placed traps in tempting places with tempting morsels. None was touched. I searched for cracks in the cement work behind the sink, the fridge, the dishwasher and the Calor gas cooker, and every tiny crack I filled with hard-setting cement … and on went the mouse activity night after night. Jeannie was distraught, and so was I.

At last, someone said: 'Have you looked in the packing of the cooker?'

I contacted my old friend Billy Bennetts at the Calor gas showroom in Penzance, and John the fitter from the showroom was sent to investigate … and, as he began to dismantle the cooker, out jumped the mouse from the packing. Luckily, it jumped into the waste-paper basket, which I covered with the *Sunday Times*, then I hastened outside and threw the cooker-loving mouse into the *escallonia* bush.

The young woman departed, and we were left to continue our celebration day. We were going to have fresh crab for lunch; a saucerful for Ambrose, and a bottle of champagne.

TEN

The following morning, I set out to repeat the walk to the Ambrose Rock. Jeannie was busy in the cottage and said she would join me later, and so I started to walk down the lane, Ambrose languidly following me until I reached Monty's Leap, where he came to a full stop. I called him; I cajoled him, but he just sat there refusing to move and so, for the first time, I was to know that he would only walk to the Ambrose Rock if Jeannie and I were together. Not once has he ever been with Jeannie on her own; not once with me.

His attitude to life had been gradually changing since Oliver died. He was like someone who has been living in the shadow of a stronger character, and who finds himself freed. He became more confident in himself, shed some of his inhibitions and, in the process, became more vulnerable and loving and, although his cat-like independence continued to dominate his behaviour, he showed in so many ways that his world revolved around ourselves. He still raced away from strangers and would not tolerate any other cat on the premises. True, he would irritate us by disappearing for hours during the day, but then, if we were sitting on the bridge, he would suddenly appear at our side and, of course, at night he would curl between us and purr. Sometimes he would break off from his purr, and give his little yap. This yap was a very special demonstration of happiness.

His appearance, ponds of dark ginger fur against light ginger, five dark ginger lines on his head between the ears, a white shirt-front, fat paws, dark ginger rings on his tail ... all these were reminders of Monty his double and now, being on his own, becoming a special character, he was often reminding us of the years we first came to Minack with Monty. No relationship, yet their lives were intertwined; so intertwined in fact that Ambrose had, by remote control, inspired a lady to research into the whereabouts of the birthplace of Monty.

The lady wrote to us, saying she was fascinated by Ambrose and Monty, and the uncanny fact that I was standing by Monty's Leap when I first saw Ambrose. Obviously, she said, she could not help me to discover exactly where Ambrose was born, but she hoped, because she lived near St Albans in Hertfordshire, she might be able to trace the birthplace of Monty.

She had given herself a formidable task. The clue as to Monty's birthplace lay in a paragraph I wrote in *A Cat in the Window*. It read:

'Jeannie's mother had an appointment at the hairdressers and she promised that immediately afterwards she would go to the pet shop to see what kittens were available. The visit never took place. At the hairdressers, she confided her mission to the girl who attended her. "But I've got a kitten that nobody wants," the girl said. "It's ginger, the last of a litter, and if we don't find a home for him by tomorrow he'll have to be put away."'

We had just married. I was at the height of my anti-cat period, yet Jeannie and her mother were plotting to inflict the presence of a cat in our new home.

The lady also had read an interview Jeannie had given in the *Hert's Advertiser*, the weekly newspaper which covers the St Albans area. Jeannie was brought up in St Albans and, in the interview, she gave the name of her mother's hairdresser as Craddocks of London Road, and the name of the then managers as Mr and Mrs Desborough.

The lady proceeded to send us reports of her investigations and we began to wonder what kind of lady she might be. Her letters were typed with the neatness of an experienced secretary, and it was obvious that her research was being conducted with a thoroughness that suggested she had a very painstaking nature. We came to the conclusion she was elderly, a devoted cat lover, who had retired after many years in an office, and who now had found a diversion in searching for Monty's birthplace. We were delighted by her interest, and felt sure that such a dedicated person would meet with success and the mystery of Monty's first home would be solved. It was not. The lady's earnest efforts produced much interesting material, but failed to find the answer; so I give a summary of the information she gleaned just in case someone who reads it may remember what happened that summer day in Craddocks of the London Road, when Monty came into our lives:

'Firstly,' wrote the lady in summary of her investigations, 'I spoke with Mrs Desborough of Craddocks (now a wine shop). She believed that Monty had been given to Mrs Nicol by Anne How who lived at Pound Farm, Sandridge, two miles out of St Albans.

'I then visited St Albans Public Library and traced from *Kelly's Directories* that in 1943 a Mr How managed the farm and Anne was his daughter. From the Directories, I discovered that Pound Farm was owned by the Salvation Army, so I contacted a Colonel Cyril Barnes to see if I could trace the present whereabouts of the daughter. Mr How, the father, was dead.

'A couple of days later, Colonel Barnes rang me to say he had discovered where Anne How now lived. Her married name was Cree and she lived at Hove, and I now thought Monty's mystery was about to be solved. Unfortunately, when I rang her she told me she left Craddocks in 1941 and, although she remembered all the names of the cats at Pound Farm, she was quite certain that Monty had not come from there.

'She did, however, remember the names of some of the girls who worked at that time at Craddocks. I traced one of them who ran a hairdressers at nearby Wheathampstead, but she couldn't help either. The names Mrs Cree gave me were Audrey Parsons, Miss Savage, Rita Simmonds, Miss Rud, Mrs Paterson, Peggy Cox and Phyllis Lane.

'I seem to have come to a dead end but, although I never did find the answer, the research was very interesting.'

The lady later wrote that she had decided to come to Cornwall and see for herself Monty's Leap and the spot where I first saw Ambrose. She had signed her letters, Hilary Richards.

Thus, there came the afternoon when we awaited the arrival of the lady whom we imagined to be elderly; a lady who had retired after many years in an office, and who had found a diversion in searching for Monty's birthplace.

Jeannie was in the garden when she saw a girl, dark, with a boyish figure, hurrying excitedly up the lane towards the cottage.

'I'm Hilary Richards!'

Jeannie looked at her in astonishment.

'You can't be! We expected an elderly lady!' And Jeannie laughed.

This pretty girl, only one year old when Monty died, had been the researcher for his birthplace.

We had to go to London a few days after the morning when Ambrose came to a full stop at Monty's Leap. The contradictions in people's lives are difficult to understand, and sometimes we look upon the behaviour of our neighbours and friends and wonder, critically, why they have done this or that. It is none of our business, of course. Yet we continue to wonder why they do not conform to the image we expect of them.

In our case, there is another side to us which gives us much pleasure, provided the experience is not prolonged. Jeannie, for instance, will always receive a special welcome from any hotel in any part of the world. The invitations she has received to stay at these hotels would make anyone wonder why she prefers to live in a cottage without a telephone, and where the well dries up in summer.

The answer lies in that we have both chosen a way of life which suits us; both of us had the luck to have success when young, so satisfying our egos and thus sparing us a greed for power. Our philosophy, I suppose, is a hope to enjoy each day, and to be aware of our fortune in living in the environment so many people wish for, and of earning enough and a little bit more.

Thus, when we go away from Minack, we always go away for a purpose, such as the occasion when I was invited to be the Castaway on 'Desert Island Discs' a programme which, over the years, has remained my radio favourite. I had so often heard on the programme excerpts of music which enchanted me and which I had never heard before ... excerpts from the eight discs which are chosen by the Castaway. Also I was always charmed by the way Roy Plomley, creator of the programme, coaxed from the Castaway revelations of his life and his character. His success lay in the fact that he always proved he had done his homework.

I had received the invitation to be the Castaway many weeks before, and I had immediately set out to do my own form of homework. It was a programme of much prestige in my own mind, and I was nervous of joining the club of fifty-two Castaways a year, who may come from any part of the world. Thus, after I had accepted the invitation, I listened even more carefully to the Castaways on the programme, hoping to learn from them. There was Gregory Peck, the Earl of Snowdon, Muhammad Ali, Pavorotti and other such names, and I became increasingly apprehensive.

It was now that Jeannie proceeded to minimise my apprehension by proposing that no trouble on our part should be spared in preparation for the day of the programme. Her theory is that any big occasion should be treated with the greatest respect and that you should aim to create an ambience which at least gives you a chance to feel at your best. The first step was to buy a tape recorder and hi-fi equipment of quality. Thus, during the weeks preceding my visit to London, I was able to spend many hours trying out the various records I thought of choosing, gauging the running times of each, and imagining replies to the sort of questions Roy Plomley might ask of me. I had a happy time sitting on the sofa, listening to the music, though I became more and more bewildered as to how I was going to choose eight discs out of all those I was playing.

Jeannie's next step was to urge me to buy a new suit. This I reluctantly proceeded to do from an old established tailor in Penzance, who showed an old world interest in my prospective purchase by asking: 'Is the suit for everyday wear, sir, or is it for special occasions?' I made my choice, and was content.

Jeannie, however, also suggested that I should have a new shirt and, without telling me, organised three elegant shirts to be delivered to me from that famous Bond Street shop, The White House. They were delivered to me, along with a selection of ties, by a director of The White House. We had met Bernard Groroby through the *Minack Chronicles*, and he had become a friend. As he was coming to Cornwall on holiday, he acted as messenger boy for my elegant shirts and ties. I chose two of the shirts and two of the ties.

I was now sartorially equipped and the time had come for the final stage in the ambience process. Jeannie, though involved as she always has been with the Savoy, enjoyed staying at Claridge's, which, of course, also comes under the umbrella of the Savoy Hotel Company, and it was to Claridge's that we travelled on the day before my appointment with Roy Plomley.

Claridge's does not seem to be like an hotel. It has the quietness of a private home. There are deep lilac carpets in the sitting rooms and dove-coloured walls, high carved ceilings and open fireplaces. It has a special aura of elegance and the rooms have period furniture, and the front hall has a wrought iron grand staircase that curves upwards from the ground floor, every gleaming brass rod polished daily. There are flower arrangements in niches in the walls, a log fire in an open fireplace in the hall, and leading into the restaurant are gilt and glass doors. In the main ballroom, where the Queen and Prince Philip attended the special evening party after the wedding of the Prince and Princess of Wales, hang the chandeliers which were bought from the Paris Exposition of 1900.

It was at Claridge's, therefore, that we arrived on the eve of

recording 'Desert Island Discs', leaving Margaret to look after Ambrose and the donkeys. I drew up outside the entrance, was greeted by Ricci the hall porter, who was to arrange for our Volvo to be taken to a garage, and then we walked through the revolving doors inside. Within a few minutes, we were being escorted by Michael Bentley, the assistant manager, to the fourth floor and to a suite overlooking the corner of Davies Street and Brook Street, with a sitting room twice the size of the floor space of the cottage. We were in the process of admiring it when the telephone bell rang and an unperturbed voice said: 'We cannot move your Volvo, sir ... there are no keys.' I had them in my pocket.

Jeannie, back in her hotel world, was of course immediately at home in the elegant atmosphere ... unlike the first time she visited Claridge's. On that occasion, a new girl in the Savoy Press Office, she was told by her boss to accompany a photographer to Claridge's where the photographer was to take the picture of the suite in which a highly important American State Department official was to stay. He was Mr Sumner Welles, and it was in the early war years and vital discussions were going to take place between him and Churchill concerning war supplies. It was necessary that he should be cosseted and the Royal Suite was prepared for him, and to his suite went the photographer and Jeannie. The photographer asked Jeannie to stand by the mantelpiece and he snapped his picture and it appeared in the evening newspaper. Unfortunately, the State Department was not amused. A pretty girl included in Mr Welles's Royal Suite? The booking was cancelled.

The recording session was the following afternoon, but first, and this again was part of Jeannie's ambience process, we were to have lunch with Roy Plomley and Derek Drescher, the producer, in the restaurant. It always amused me to watch Jeannie acting as hostess in glamorous surroundings; one day in her tiny galley of a kitchen; the next day at Claridge's, with Bruno, the maitre d'hotel, and others like Luigi, Tony and Hassan caring for her as if she were a queen. There we were, Roy Plomley, Derek Drescher, who blends the interviews into programme length, and ourselves, and hoping that we would find in each other a *rapport*.

It is strange how with some people one is immediately in sympathy, while with other people one seems to be separated by an invisible brick wall. I meet someone for a few minutes and I feel I have known them all my life. Others I have known for years and yet I am unable to communicate with them. Some people spark me; others make me feel dreary. Some people by their sulky manner can ruin a day; other people through their joy of living can enhance it. There is no logical explanation for these contradictions, though they suggest, whatever the political theorists may wish, that a rational society in which everyone has a digital part to play can never be created. The vagaries of human nature will always prevail.

Roy Plomley is a gentle person, shy even, and I was to find he was one of those people in whose company one felt immediately at ease. He created 'Desert Island Discs' in 1941, when the BBC engaged it for eight programmes, and it has been running ever since. He is not, however, just the presenter of 'Desert Island Discs'. He was in the theatre and, as a playwright, he has had over fourteen professional plays produced. The first volume of his autobiography, *Days Seemed Longer*, describes his early days when he was connected with commerical broadcasting based in Europe, and how he was caught in the fall of Paris in 1940, where he had just married a beautiful Chinese dancer. They live now on the riverside at Putney.

So by the time lunch was over, and Jeannie's ambience process was reaching its climax, Roy Plomley had become a friend and, although I was naturally nervous, I was not in a panic. We reached Broadcasting House, Jeannie coming with us, proceeded to walk along the labyrinth of corridors, and finally reached a box of a room divided from the control room by a glass panel. Behind this panel were to sit Jeannie and Derek Drescher, the producer. In the box of a room sat Roy Plomley, a record player on the table to his left, a collection of the records I had chosen also on the table; and opposite him, in a utility office chair, a mike on a table between us, I sat. A red light shone and the programme had begun and when, three hours later, we were back in Claridge's and having a drink, I told him about Jeannie's ambience process.

'A new tape recorder, new hi-fi equipment, a new suit, a new shirt and tie, a suite at Claridge's,' I said, 'that is how I was led to my Desert Island!'

He signed a copy of the first volume of his autobiography *Days Seemed Longer*, with the words: 'To my new friends, Jeannie and Derek, with gratitude and every good wish.'

It was a happy day.

The records I chose were as follows:

1. 'The Shepherd boy's song' which begins Act III of Puccini's *Tosca*. I invented friends when I was a boy and one of these friends was the shepherd boy who sang this song as he tended his sheep at dawn in the hills above Rome.

2. *Reflets dans l'eau* by Debussy, the piano imagery of water which I used to play on the Welte, an electrical piano player, with lights out, as I sat in our one-time family home of Glendorgal near Newquay in Cornwall. I used to sit there, gazing up the darkness of the north coast to the winking light of Trevose Lighthouse. It was played by Walter Gieseking.

3. The Gallop from Bizet's *Jeux d'Enfants* because I will always remember the night I first saw the young dancers of the Ballet Russe ... Lichine, Toumanova, Baronova. There were five of us in the party: only I survived the War.

4. 'Jeannie with the Light Brown Hair' by Stephen Foster. Carroll Gibbons used to play this when he saw Jeannie coming into the Savoy Restaurant. Amazingly, Derek Drescher's secretary discovered in the BBC archives a record of Carroll Gibbons himself playing this haunting melody.

5. The Adagio from Rachmaninov's Second Symphony played by the London Symphony Orchestra conducted by André Previn. A wonderful symphony.
6. The finale of Haydn's String Quartet in D Major Op. 76 No. 5 played by the Amadeus Quartet. I was late in appreciating chamber music. This particular work has a marvellous, exciting beat.
7. The Prelude to Grieg's Holberg Suite Op. 40 and played by the Northern Sinfonia Orchestra conducted by Paul Tortelier.
8. 'This Is My Lovely Day', music by Vivian Ellis and lyrics by A. P. Herbert, sung by Georges Guetary and Lizbeth Webb. I heard this song for the first time at the memorable first night of *Bless The Bride* at the Adelphi Theatre.

Roy Plomley also asked the usual two questions. What luxury would I like to take with me to my Desert Island? And what book?

I asked for an astral telescope with which to study the stars as the luxury; and I chose Marcel Proust's *Remembrance of Things Past* as the book. I chose Proust's great work because of his influence on me. I was nineteen when I was advised to read *Swanns Way*, the first volume; and suddenly I discovered that my secret thoughts and doubts were not unique. From that moment I have seldom read a book without hoping that in the text there will be some message, some form of self-awakening, that will help to enlighten me in the manner of my living.

And for the record to take with me to my Desert Island, I chose the Adagio of Rachmaninov's Second Symphony.

We were back at the cottage by eight o'clock the following evening. Rain had begun to fall as we crossed in the darkness from Devonshire into Cornwall; first a spatter, then as we swept past Launceston and on to Bodmin Moor it began to lash the Volvo.

'Hold on, Ambrose ...' Jeannie was saying in her coming-home routine; 'We won't be long, Ambrose.'

We imagined him waiting, wondering whether he had another night alone.

'Hold on, Ambrose.'

We raced along the Bodmin by-pass, then on the road to Goss Moor and Fraddon and through Mitchell.

'Thank God it's all over, Jeannie,' I said.

Down the hill to Bridgewater, past Redruth and Camborne, then down steep, curving Roseworthy Hill and up the other side to Connor Downs and Hayle.

'Less than an hour, Ambrose!'

Along the Lelant causeway to Cockwells, Crowlas, and then that stretch of road that suddenly opens up the whole sweep of Penzance Bay with St Michael's Mount to one's left, Newlyn in the distance, and Penzance ahead, welcoming you like an old friend.

We passed through Penzance along the promenade, across Newlyn Bridge and up Paul Hill, through Sheffield and the telephone box which we use as if it were a home telephone, and on to Lamorna Turn, then up Boleigh Hill until at last we reached our lane, and Jeannie called out: 'We're home, Ambrose!' Still a mile to go.

I drew up outside the cottage and switched off the engine but, instead of silence, there was the sound of fury in the trees. The rain was lashing them and the gale, a gale from the south, was tearing through them and, when I opened the car door, it was pushed back on me.

'What a night to return on,' I said, finding the torch in the back and giving it to Jeannie. 'You go ahead,' I said. And she got out of the car and, head down to the rain and the gale, went up the path calling: 'Ambrose! Ambrose!'

All true animal lovers behave in the same way. Their love is so profound that they do not mind how foolish they may appear to cool-headed onlookers. Holidaymakers can be particularly foolish. The best moment of their holidays is when they are reunited with their cats in catteries, dogs in kennels.

I followed Jeannie into the cottage and, as I entered, I heard her cries of endearment and I was immediately thankful that Ambrose was not playing the role of a vexed cat, a cat who had decided to ignore the inside of the cottage, preferring instead the discomfort of some outhouse in order to bring misery to us on our return.

'Where was he?' I asked.

'He's still there ... look, he's on the bed.'

I looked through the doorway into our tiny bedroom and there was Ambrose, curled on one of my shirts, left by Jeannie on the bed when we left for London so that it would remind him of us. He blinked at me, then stretched and jumped to the floor and strolled towards us.

'So you're back,' he seemed to be saying: 'I've had a most restful time while you've been away. Nobody has picked me up; I've had the bed to myself with no legs in the way, and Margaret has catered for me admirably.'

There were the donkeys for me now to see.

Have you ever heard a donkey hooting in the roar of a gale? The first time I heard this was during the night after Penny had died and Fred was spending his first night alone. I had left him in the field above the cottage, and this field at the far end led to a bulb meadow, and through a narrow section of this bulb meadow to the wood. That night after Penny had died, a January night, I went out after dinner to find Fred. It was raining and a gale was blowing, just like this night on our return from London. I went up from the cottage to the big field and, above the noise of the storm, I heard in the distance this cry of great distress, and the sound of it hurt me for it was the cry of Fred who had suddenly realised he was alone. I hurried across the field, found him inside the wood, and I did not leave him for an hour or more.

On this occasion, I left Jeannie and Ambrose together, for Jeannie had sat down in the armchair and Ambrose was now on her lap, purring. I went outside and down towards the stable field and, once again, I heard the hooting of Fred in a gale. No sadness this time, for Merlin, silent Merlin, Merlin who had never been granted the gift of a hoot, was his devoted companion. This time, it was a hoot of greeting. In the darkness, in the roar of the storm, he was standing by the fence in front of the stables, hullabalooing our return. Before I went to them, I had taken off the jacket of my London suit and put on an oiler, and I had also collected a handful of chocolate biscuits. They were waiting, white noses in the dark, and I let myself in through the gate and they followed me out of the storm into the stillness of the stable. Munch, munch, and when the biscuits were consumed, I stood there with them while Fred, as was his habit after eating chocolate biscuits, proceeded to lick my hand. Lunchtime at Claridge's; evening in the shelter of the stable. Normality was returning.

When I left them, I forced myself to walk down the lane, my torch beaming the way, so as to inspect the greenhouses in the field on the other side of Monty's Leap. Always this worry in a gale that the greenhouses are being damaged. I turned into the field and from a distance, in case of flying glass, I shone the torch around each of the three green-houses, along the sides, along the roofs and, to my relief, I saw no gaps, no panes that were smashed. Then I went back to inspect the Orlyt and here again I saw no obvious signs of damage. It was when I saw the small greenhouse, the one where, in spring, we bunch the daffoldils, that I had a shock. One of the roof frames had come adrift and, although the glass was still intact, I realised it would soon break up if it were left while the gale roared on.

I did not think of the risk I was taking. I just knew that, unless I stopped the slipping of the frame, a huge gap would appear in the greenhouse and the gale swirling inside would disintegrate it; so I set about trying to wedge the frame back into its original position. First I put the torch on the ground so that it was pointing upwards, shining on the frame. Then, after contemplating how to deal with the situation for a minute or two, I fetched a rake from where we keep the garden tools and, with the rake against the frame, I pushed it inch by inch back into position. Leaves were flying like confetti from the surrounding elms as I did so, and there was a crash behind me, and I realised the galvanised top of the dustbin had been blown off. I now had to fix the frame so that it did not slide back again, and I picked up the torch and went inside the greenhouse and collected a hammer and nails. This was my trickiest task. I had to hammer the nails partly into the wood at the top of the side frame, then bend the nails over so that they held the sliding frame, anyhow for the time being. I succeeded, and I was pleased with myself when I collected the torch and returned to the cottage.

'*Where* have you been?' asked Jeannie.

I explained.

'You really are silly.'

'It had to be done.'

'But not at night after a long journey and in a roaring gale!'

Ambrose brought calm to the situation. I had sat down on the sofa, and he had jumped on my lap.

'Anyhow,' I said, 'nothing matters now we're home.'

'Quite right,' said Jeannie. 'Nothing.'

We got up late the following morning and the gale had died away; it was still, and the sun shone through our bedroom window. When I had dressed, I went outside to the bridge and the air was full of the scent of wet earth and the ozone from the sea, unsullied purity of the countryside. A late Red Admiral butterfly fluttered on the *escallonia* bush, a dazzling colour against the leafy dark green. A robin sang its wistful autumn song among the blackthorn to my right. A bee settled momentarily on the tired mignonette in front of me. There was the sound of curlews calling in the distance and, on the other side of the valley, on Oliver land, a cock pheasant suddenly cackled, followed a split second later by the distant double boom of the French Concorde on its morning run to

New York. The cock pheasant was probably Phineas. I do not know. When Jeannie gives a name to a pheasant, or a gull, or a chaffinch, only those with special characteristics can we identify for sure. Such as the evening gull, for instance, who arrives on our roof day after day, week after week, month after month, as dusk is falling, and waits there, silhouetted against the dying sky, until we feed him.

I stood there on the bridge, happy that I was back in a world of uncontrived pleasures where the senses come into their own. So much knowledge is pumped into us that imagination becomes dulled. We are filled with information and expert opinions, and rules based on theory supersede instinct based on experience in the making of decisions. We reach the stage when we look, but do not feel. We live along the surface of life, then wonder why inner satisfaction eludes us.

Of course, there are those who will say it is nonsensical to romanticise the simple pleasures in times of great economic distress. We have, however, always been in periods of great economic distress. Generations have been promised the Utopia which is never reached, and yet there is this pressure put upon us by elitist groups to make us feel foolish if we enjoy uncontrived pleasures. Such people seem to think it is better to knock than to build; to destroy confidence in established standards; to exploit the sordid rather than the virtues, and often to create controversies regardless of the truth. In the struggle for notoriety and financial survival, they daily search for sensation at the expense of integrity. Perhaps they are the necessary ingredients of progress, and this I can understand. I refuse, however, to believe that they contribute to the happiness of those who are seeking peace of mind within themselves.

Rabindranath Tagore wrote many years ago:

'The west seems to take a pride in thinking that it is subduing nature, as if we are living in a hostile world

154

where we have to wrest everything we want from an unwilling and alien arrangement of things. This sentiment is the produce of the city-wall habit and training of mind. For in the city life, man naturally directs the concentrated light of his mental vision upon his own life and works, and this creates an artificial dissociation between himself and the Universal Nature within whose bosom he lies.'

An ideal world would perhaps have everyone living in isolated sections of the countryside, self-supporting, at one with the wild animals, and feeling free. But it will never be an ideal world, and those who live in the country sometimes now find themselves living a form of the city-wall habit that Tagore describes. The gap that divides the city life-country life conception has so narrowed over the years that country life is scarcely separated in many cases from city life. Cheap living no longer exists. Country cottages fetch city prices, and become holiday homes for city-orientated people. Rough country manners have been smoothed. Spontaneous pleasures, in contrast to the organised pleasures of the tourist, are becoming rare.

I left the bridge and my musings, and walked over to the old-fashioned sink that serves as the donkey water trough in the field above the cottage. An extension from the pipe of the tank at the top of the well feeds the sink when I turn on the tap. Often in autumn there is a severe shortage of well water, and we get our supply from another well source. I will not explain how this is done because I have tried to explain the method to Jeannie many times, and yet it still remains beyond her comprehension. So I hope you will accept the fact that, on this occasion, I was collecting water from our second well. I arrived at the old-fashioned sink, found it nearly empty, and turned on the tap to refill it; then walked away because I thought I could use the refilling period by doing something more useful than watching it fill up. I thereupon went into the porch, sat down at the table, and began writing out a list of the tasks which lay ahead of us.

There was the Q.E.2 field to motor scythe, where grow the Hollywood and Dutch Master ... four meadows in the Merlin cliff, so called because it was here that Merlin had his first sight of the *Scillonian* passing by, and which had to be cut down with my brush cutter ... the greenhouses had to be cleared; one of the old tomato plants, another of an assortment of cucumber and marrow plants, of runner beans and sweet peas, another of the branches of the Cape goose-berries, and all of them of prolific weeds ... there were still blackberries to pick for the freezer, and sloes for the sloe gin ... a bonfire was necessary to dispose of the backlog of Sunday newspapers ... much garden work waited to be done around the cottage ... the inside of the cottage needed to be painted ... Christmas cards had to be organised ... and over on the other side of the valley exploration awaited us, paths to be created, advice from the Cornwall Naturalist Society and the Conservation Trust obtained, and the decision to be made as to what to do with the land.

I was still adding to this list when there was a call from Jeannie in the kitchen:

'No water coming through the tap!'

'Oh, my God! I exclaimed.

And I rushed out to the donkey trough. I had forgotten it. The trough was overflowing. The tank had been drained.

Later that morning I saw Walter Grose, my old friend the farmer, whom I once called the Pied Piper of cats because he had so many. He has only one now. I told him of my foolishness, and he looked at me wryly, said nothing for a moment, then:

'Too much of a hurry. That's what comes of going to London. ... In the old days, those down Minack would have walked up the lane with a pitcher and filled it from the well and walked back. Taking their time, they would have done.

But you,' he said, and he was smiling, 'couldn't even wait by the tap which was doing the work for you.'

ELEVEN

It requires five days, I have found, for me to recover my rhythm of country life after I have been away. Lack of self-discipline, no doubt, but it remains a fact that for five days I will dither. I will look at my desk and move a pile of papers from one side of the desk to the other. I may go up to the greenhouse, where the tomatoes have grown during the summer, begin pulling up the old plants but, after pulling up a dozen, I will stop. I will weed the garden for ten minutes, then pause and look out to sea, and let my mind wander. I will decide to wash the car, then fail to do so. I will sit on the sofa, puffing at my pipe, watching Jeannie active in the kitchen, and feel guilty, and yet do nothing to remove my sense of guilt. I am disorientated. I am cross with myself, and I am only thankful that my visit away is behind me and there is not to be another one in the foreseeable future.

Two days, three days, four days and the rhythm of country life was enveloping me again. I said to Jeannie on the morning of the fifth day that I was going to take out the Condor and continue cutting a path from where I had stopped at the Ambrose Rock, and I actually did so. I filled the tank with petrol, started the engine and set off. I reached the Ambrose Rock and began roaring away through the bracken and brambles, gripping the handlebars as the Condor plunged this way and that and, as always, it would come to a noisy full stop when the blades hit a hidden group of stones. Once it was bogged down in a particularly dense patch of undergrowth, and I had to heave it clear. As I did so, I saw that a bramble had torn my hand, and I fumbled for a handkerchief and wrapped it round my hand. No curses from me. I was enjoying myself. The rhythm of country life had returned.

So too had the urge to discuss the future.

'Jeannie,' I said later that day. 'I admit I was wrong.'

'What about?'

She was sitting in the porch, Ambrose lying on the chair opposite her, and she was drawing him.

'About expanding with more bulbs ... using the new land for more bulbs.'

'I always thought it a fantasy idea.'

'Sad, though.'

'Sad, yes, but it's simply not worth it. We would never get the money back on the bulb outlay, and we would be pouring out money on wages and freight costs and so on.'

'Anyhow,' I said, 'the Minack bulbs have been doing well and here it is not half-way through October and I've got all the meadows cut down.'

'Think what we've saved in wages by you doing it yourself.' Jeannie paused.

'I want to ask you something ... why is it that so many politicians and union leaders denounce the unemployment figures without analysing the cause of them?'

'It puzzles me, too.'

'They condemn the unemployment figures, but never admit one of the basic reasons for them,' went on Jeannie. 'Take ourselves. We once had two girls working for us and a man. Today, with insurance, three such people would be costing £12,000 a year. I mean it is ludicrous ... and when you set that kind of wage figure for business all over the country, it is so painfully obvious why there is unemployment. ... Anyhow,' said Jeannie and, all the while we had been talking, she had continued to draw Ambrose, 'like lots and lots of other people, we are much, much happier doing the work ourselves.'

Ambrose stirred, stretched and jumped to the floor.

'Oh, Ambrose,' said Jeannie, 'if you'd stayed there another minute, I would have finished.'

My life with Jeannie has never been dull. We have been happy in each other's company because we have not followed the conventional rules. A close relationship is the basis of a happy marriage, but a rigid one is not. A rigid relationship is usually the cause of marriage disaster, for it results in frustration and this, in turn, produces accusations of over-possessiveness. If two people have found they share the same attitude to life, an attitude which is intuitive, then it is foolish to be over-possessive. It is part of the fun of a happy marriage to pretend you are both independent, but that there is always a harbour to return to.

Another effect of my life with Jeannie is that we talk too much to each other. It is a consequence of two people living in a cottage without a telephone, who have no permanent neighbours within casual visiting distance, who share each other's interests. Comments flow about politics; overpaid footballers; slow drivers who hog the road, refusing to let following cars pass; the winning performer of the Leeds Piano Festival; Geoffrey Boycott (in Jeannie's view, he can do no wrong); yet another reading of a Brontë book; the dedication of athletes in training; the profound sense of loving in a Charles Morgan novel; the strange law compelling the publication of Wills after a person has kept his financial affairs secret all his life; our admiration for Gwen John and our dislike of Picasso, except for his Blue Period ... all this, and trivial talk.

Such as this.

'Can I speak?' Jeannie asks.

I am at the moment engrossed in the third chapter of Raleigh Trevelyan's *Rome, 1944.*

'Yes,' I reply, absentmindedly.

'Elizabeth Taylor is coming to do a play in London.'

'Yes?'

'I was thinking of the time I first met her at the Savoy, and *so* spoilt by her mother.'

No word from me.

'I'm trying to finish the chapter,' I said, shifting in my corner of the sofa. 'It's a fascinating book.'

Or the interruption is the other way round.

'Jeannie,' I say, 'I must read you this.'

An item from John Junor's column in the *Sunday Express*.

'In a minute, I'm trying to finish this letter.'

We each have wood cabins away from the cottage. Jeannie's cabin stands within the roofless stone walls of an ancient building once used to house farm implements. She writes there and paints, and on the walls hang her pictures and drawings. From the window she can look out across the moorland to Carn Barges and the sea and, close to the entrance, there is a wire fence, the other side of which is a favourite place of the donkeys. They are sheltered there when the rains come in from the south, and they will stand, bottoms facing the fence, making Jeannie feel sorry for them as she sits in the warmth of her cabin. Ambrose often joins her there and, though flattered by his presence, he also can cause her inconvenience. Ambrose is apt to suffer from claustrophobia, and so she has to leave the door ajar and this can be chilly for her.

My own cabin is beneath high ash trees. My window looks out onto a small clearing, a patch of untidy grass where clumps of the Star of Bethlehem flower in the spring. Immediately in front, against the high bank and stone wall which separates the donkey field from the wood, is an elder, among the branches of which I will watch a wren hopping, or a blue tit, or a robin, diverting me. A little to the right is a magnolia I planted, but which seldom flowers; perhaps it is too much in the shadow of the ash trees. An occasional rabbit lollops through the grass and, in the spring, when my door is open, the cabin is scented by a nearby hawthorn and by the Sunrise daffodils which I once threw at random in the wood. I call the cabin Joybells, and the reason for this is that, soon after it was erected, we visited Jeannie's ninety-four year old uncle, the ebullient Canon Martin Andrews, author of *Canon's Folly*, at a time when I was for some reason depressed.

'Oh, don't be depressed,' he said. 'Life is all joy bells, joy bells!'

I have another place away from the cottage, which I call my confusion room. Nobody is allowed in it. It is, in fact, the other half of the stables and so, when I am in it, I can hear through the wall, when they are there, the shuffling of donkey hooves. The confusion room is where I face up to the bills and deal with my letters and have a filing cabinet, and where the table is littered with odd articles such as pipes and magazines with the word 'Keep' on the front, and such things as a telescope, last season's daffodil invoice book, numerous photographs, a barometer which belonged to my father, empty tobacco tins, coins, nails, paper clips, envelopes, and so on. Then behind, as I sit at the table, is a mass of books collected over the years which I would have in the cottage if there were space; and there is a higgledy-piggledy pile of old mono records; and there is a mattress leaning against the back wall, and a cupboard containing clothes against another wall; and there is a wine rack and suit-cases, one on top of the other; two or three in travelling use, two or three others used as storage containers of letters, newspapers, magazines concerning both our lives; and there is of course LABOUR WARMS. This massive teak cupboard which dominated my nursery at 48 Bramham Gardens, Kensington, has the words in bold black type: LABOUR WARMS, SLOTH HARMS. It holds a further vast amount of documents relating to the past . . . and I wrote about some of these documents in *Sun On The Lintel*. I respect my confusion room and its contents. Understandably, however, I prefer my cabin under the ash trees.

'I tell you what I'll do,' I said to Jeannie, after we had both agreed that bulb expansion was impossible. 'I'll write to the Cornwall Naturalists' Trust and explain we want Oliver land to be a nature reserve and see what advice they can give.'

Philip Blamey and Majorie Blamey, the famous illustrator of wild plants and flowers, are key figures in the Trust, which was formed in 1962, and they work energetically on its behalf. The object is to safeguard the wild areas of Cornwall, to study the ecological background of such areas, to acquire if possible such areas by purchase or gift, and always be ready to outline the case for preservation to the authorities when such areas are threatened by a planning application. One becomes a member of the Trust by writing to its headquarters at Trelissick near Truro.

'The trouble about nature reserves,' said Jeannie, 'is that they often seem to be designed for the benefit of human beings instead of for the inhabitants. I mean they are sort of zoos.'

'That's because there's this tremendous thirst for knowledge about nature as an antidote to modern living,' I replied.

'I understand that . . . but I can't accept the attitude of those who refuse to treat nature as a form of magic. Too much seeking after knowledge, it seems to me, takes away magic. Too many people visiting beautiful places do the same.'

'I suppose the twitchers I heard about the other day come into that category,' I said. 'Funny name, twitchers. I wonder how it came into the language.'

Twitchers are birdwatchers who, when they hear of the

presence of a rare bird, will travel hundreds of miles to try and catch a sight of it. They will swarm over the land where the rare bird has been seen, scores of them, binoculars at the ready, caring not for the trampled land of the unfortunate owner. Twitchers can be a nuisance.

I have a friend who is pilot of the British Airways helicopter between Penzance and the Scillies and who is a keen dry fly fisherman of trout in the Drift reservoir near Penzance. The route of the helicopter normally takes him over the reservoir and, when he is on his last flight of the day, and it is the appropriate time of the year, he will glance down at the reservoir and, if it appears sparse of other fishermen, he will take his rod there on his way back home to Sennen. He enjoys being solitary. He does not enjoy fishing in the mass.

One day he looked down from his helicopter, saw no fishermen around the reservoir, and decided he would pay a visit for a couple of hours. He had been on the bank for a while, casting his line, content with his thoughts, when suddenly he became aware that he was no longer alone. A group of people with binoculars had appeared not far away and were watching him. He was embarrassed. Why should these people be interested in his fishing methods? And anyhow their presence took away the pleasure of the fishing … his solitude.

At last he walked to the nearest gentleman with binoculars and enquired why he, and the others, found him of such interest.

'Not interested in you,' replied the gentleman. 'It's a Phalarope we're watching in the water close to you. A rare visitor to these parts.'

My friend gave up his fishing and went home.

Twitchers, however praiseworthy their interest in one aspect of nature, reflect an unsettling feature of this age. They reflect those who descend upon beautiful places and who, by doing so, destroy the peace which solitude provides. Solitude, indeed, is becoming an embarrassing word. Lone, beautiful places, the argument runs, should be opened up for everyone and individuals who seek solitude should be forced away and a noisy crowd take their place. People feel safe in a crowd. Being in a crowd is a form of dope. But a crowd will never lead us to the peace of mind we seek. Solitude is required for this. Beautiful places, unspoilt by the many.

Cats, of course, also enjoy solitude, but they do not have to concern themselves with philosophical theories. Their philosophy is a sensible one. Always act independently. Such a philosophy will cause trouble on many occasions and, although I am always ready to forgive Ambrose, there are times when he vexes me.

Certain situations which vex me will be familiar to many people who share their lives with a cat. Always the live present, which is brought indoors. My love for Ambrose turns into wrath as, on hands and knees, I search for the present under the bookcase, behind the pile of records, beneath the sofa.

Other vexing situations which will be familiar include the daytime disappearance trick when I want to show him off; the night-time obduracy in being deaf to my call to come in; and, as we all know, the digging of holes in the garden. This October, after difficulty in growing wallflower plants during the summer, we had planted our few successes in a bed at the corner of the cottage which Ambrose passed every day on the way to his day quarters in the Orlyt. Unfortunately, it was his favourite dig-a-hole spot, and thus I would find him there, paw vigorously digging with abandon, and Jessie Matthews' song would come into my mind with a word variation: 'Over my shoulder goes one wallflower; over my shoulder goes another!'

Apart from the dig-a-hole spot being on the way to his day quarters, it was also on the way to the apple house where, in order to escape the aroma of the boiling coley, we had a Calor gas camp stove on which the fish could boil. We were spared, therefore, the aroma. Ambrose, on the other hand, had every chance to enjoy it while he sat beside the stove waiting for the cooking to be completed, and this was an occasion when he did not vex us. He was most helpful. Indeed, Jeannie called him her assistant chef because he was so solicitous about the boiling of the fish that, if she became absorbed in some other task and momentarily forgot the boiling fish, Ambrose would come hurrying out of the apple house in obvious distress, declaiming by his manner: 'It's boiling over! My coley is boiling over!'

He had to wait, of course, until it cooled and the wait was punctuated by impatient yaps. Then Jeannie mixed puppy biscuits with the coley because it is good for the teeth and she placed the saucer on the floor and Ambrose quickly emptied it, and off he would go to sleep off the feast in some chosen corner. Strangely, he seldom came indoors during the daytime. Only after dark did he join us.

On sunny days, even in winter, we will often have a sandwich lunch outdoors, and we will sit on the bridge or, if the wind is a northerly, we will go round to a corner which looks out over the Q.E.2 field. The sun shines into this corner, and a wall and a few blackthorns shelter us. Since Ambrose would often suddenly arrive to join us, we would wonder how he had known we were there and, one day, we decided to make an experiment to discover whether it really was a case of extra-sensory powers.

The day in question was in early December. An airliner on the way from Europe to America traced a white plume above us in the blue sky; across the Bay the line of the Lizard was pencil-sharp clear and we could see the mushroom dishes of the Goonhilly Satellite Station. We sat on the bench in our corner, safe from the northerly, the sun warming us as if on a spring day.

Ambrose had had his fill of coley and we had seen him walk off to the small greenhouse, jump up on the bench and settle himself in the far end, surrounded by paraphernalia such as empty cardboard boxes and old newspapers. Thus, knowing he was there, at least two hundred yards away, and asleep, we began enjoying our sandwiches.

Then I said, jokingly:

'Let's play a game of willing Ambrose to come to us!'

'If you like.'

We put our heads in our hands and began to concentrate our thoughts on Ambrose. A minute or two later, I heard Jeannie murmuring:

'You're stirring ... you are thinking of us ... you are stretching ... you are walking along the bench ... you have jumped down ... you are passing the rose garden, passing the cottage ...'

Suddenly, round to our corner, came Amrose.

'Jeannie,' I called out in astonishment, 'it's worked!'

Ambrose, for me, has become a talisman, and if I wake up in the middle of the night, worrying about something, and Ambrose is on the bed, probably at the bottom of the bed, so pinioning the movement of my legs, I will feel impelled to put out a hand and touch his soft coat, fearing that if I did not do so my worry might materialise into reality. The touch reassures me. I feel I will be free of my worry in the morning.

I still marvel how it is that he does not catch birds. He is like his predecessors, Monty, Lama and Oliver. Probably it is due to the hunting available, mice galore and rabbits. I would hate it if Ambrose were a bird hunter, and sometimes I have wondered unnecessarily what my reaction would have been if he were a bird catcher. Perhaps I would have consoled myself with the view of a cat lover I know, who claims that cats catching birds belong to the cycle of nature, and that they are sharing, along with hawks, magpies, carrion crows, nature's task of achieving a population balance of birds, and that they are doing a form of culling.

I can, however, understand the rage of those who see a cat catch a bird. I do not, on the other hand, understand the attitude of some bird fanciers. I have never had a wish to be a part of their world in which exotic coloured birds from every continent, from every remote jungle corner, are transported to European areas and incarcerated in pens for their owners to gaze at, and treat commercially, buying and selling, as if they were tins on a shop's shelf.

Such people, I have learnt, will trap cats, then kill them. Some will shoot any cat which comes in the vicinity of their aviaries. Mind you, the exotic birds imprisoned within their wire-mesh prisons are in no danger from the cat. The cat will never be able to reach them. But the bird fancier vests a Freudian hate for each cat he sees, and gains satisfaction by killing it. No thought of the person who loved the cat. No thought of the agonising distress suffered by that person. No thought how that person will always wonder what had happened.

December produces Christmas card activity, and one of the purposes, I remember, of our sandwich lunch, when we willed Ambrose to join us, was to discuss the sending out of our Christmas cards.

It is a melancholy aspect of life that friends disappear. There you are, at some period of your life, enjoying the fun and intimacy of friendship, half believing it will go on forever and then circumstances take you away and the fun is ended; not by dying, but the separation leading to a new range of life. I often think of those to whom I said goodbye, optimistically thinking I would see them again, but never have done so, and often I have wished to wave a wand and bring them back into my life. Christmas cards at least help to preserve a tenuous connection with some. They are worth the effort and expense for this reason, and this year we decided to have a photograph of a meadow of open daffoldils down Minack cliff to serve as this tenuous connection.

The Christmas cards we receive we stick along the beams of the cottage. I stand on a ladder and Jeannie pushes the drawing pins through the Christmas cards and hands them to me. Sometimes I ask for a small size one; sometimes a large size one, according to the spaces available on the beams.

There is a rush of excitement performing this task as one looks at a Christmas card, memorises who sent it, so that in the time over Christmas you can look and say that you remember the last time you saw the sender. A sentimental time.

There is holly around the cottage. Down Minack cliff, past the little cave where we first saw Oliver curled there as a kitten, is a holly bush perched above a drop to the sea below. There have never been any berries on this holly bush, but the crackling leaves are a deep green and, ever since we discovered it years ago, this holly bush has been our source of holly for the cottage.

It has a rival now and, although we will always continue to make the annual pilgrimage down Minack cliff and carry holly back to the cottage in a wicker basket, we will also be collecting holly from the rival. The rival is on Oliver land. I had discovered it while I was plunging through the undergrowth with the Condor.

Thus one day, a few days before Christmas, Jeannie said to me that it was time to collect the cottage holly and first we went in the customary way down Minack cliff; then, with a feeling of pride, we went off to the holly bush I had newly discovered, and we had a surprising companion. It was not Ambrose; it was not the donkeys; it was Ron the rook.

On this occasion, Ron behaved out of character. Instead of his customary use of us as a meal ticket, he left the roof and proceeded to follow us down the lane. He flew to an elm tree above Monty's Leap and, when we had crossed Monty's Leap and had gone further up the lane, he proceeded to wheel in the sky above us and, after crossing the Clover field, then on to the Ambrose Rock, we found him again above us. Collecting holly with a rook observing us enhanced the pleasure of preparing for Christmas.

The Christmas tree, lit with coloured lights, stands in the porch on the right as you come in through the door. It is a small Christmas tree, and it is placed on top of the boot cupboard. It is always much admired, because as you come

169

round the corner of the cottage at night the lights are
greeting you through the glass of the porch. This Christmas,
it had a most unusual admirer. On a Monday, a pigeon had
suddenly appeared outside the cottage door, a very tame

pigeon, which greedily pecked up the bird seed I threw on the
ground, apart from drinking the water in the bowl I put
beside him. It is not unusual for us to have wayward racing
pigeons during the spring and summer, pigeons which have
become bored with the race and decided to have time off.
They may stay with us for a few days and then off they go. We
have never before, however, had a pigeon visiting us at
Christmas, and a pigeon which had no rings of identification.

Since he had come on a Monday, he was called Monday. He
was a blue chequer and his friendliness was such that
Ambrose viewed him with astonishment. He would be
outside the door in the morning, having the cheek to block

Ambrose's way, and Ambrose would watch him with deep suspicion then, as if he were scared, would dash up the two steps into the front garden. Monday was unperturbed. Monday treated it as his right that he should be at Minack and behave as if he were the boss and expect us to pander to his every need.

He was indeed a most extraordinary bird for he had complete trust in us, although we were strangers to him and, as I watched him, it went through my mind how such trust can easily be exploited. A human being will trust another, only to find he has been betrayed. A pigeon will trust a cat, the wrong cat, not a cat with an Ambrose nature, and lose his life.

However, what intrigued Jeannie and me was Monday's roosting habit. Visiting pigeons usually fly away at dusk, or find a perch in the barn. Monday had different ideas. He decided his evening perch should be on the glass roof of the porch, sheltered a little by the gutter . . . and directly over the Christmas tree. Hence at night with the tree lit, we would look up and see two beady eyes watching us. It was an uncanny way of enjoying our Christmas dinner. It was worrying too because the weather was rough over Christmas and the rains sprayed the glass roof, and we saw Monday huddling closer to the feeble protection of the gutter. Monday left us after we had had a happy Boxing Day party. The party must have upset him. He was gone in the morning.

On Christmas Eve, there had been the ceremony of the mince-pies. The ceremony originated from the convincing story of an old Cornishman we met at the Engine Inn at Cripplease not far from St Ives. He swore to us that donkeys always knelt at midnight on Christmas Eve, and so Jeannie and I began a tradition which was inspired by the old man's story. Our original idea was to wait until midnight to see if the donkeys really did kneel but, the first time, we lost our nerve, and we decided to leave it as a mystery. So we departed a few minutes before midnight.

Every Christmas Eve when Penny was alive we performed

this ceremony, always leaving before midnight. I used to light a candle, fixed in an old-fashioned candle-stick, and its quavering light lit up the rough white walls of the stable as Penny and Fred jostled each other for the mince-pies, homemade by Jeannie, and which she held above their white noses. The last time Penny and Fred jostled each other, when I tried to light the candle it suddenly dived up in a flame, then collapsed in a wax mess. It was an age old warning. Sadness was coming. Penny died a week later. The collapsed candle is still there on the sill of the ivy-framed window facing the lane. I have never moved it since that last mince-pie party with Penny and Fred.

Merlin's first introduction to a mince-pie was not a success. He spat it out. Indeed, that first Christmas Eve after Penny died was a disaster because Fred firmly refused to come into the stable. However, the ceremony has now been successfully resumed, except that it is performed by torchlight and we no longer wait till close to midnight. We join the donkeys after Christmas Eve dinner, and Merlin now vies with Fred for the mince-pies as eagerly as Penny did.

It began to rain on this particular Christmas Eve as we stood in the stable, and when we returned to the cottage and I looked up to see Monday in the light of the Christmas tree, huddled against the gutter, I suddenly felt he was a symbol of lonely people everywhere. Foolish to feel a touch of sadness on such a happy occasion. Or is a feeling like that a blessing? A warning not to take happiness for granted.

Inside the cottage, Jeannie filled two liqueur glasses with our homemade sloe gin, and she raised her glass.

'Happy Christmas!'

'Happy Christmas!'

Ambrose was curled on the sofa and, as we stood there, he put a paw over his eyes, blocking the light. He was wanting us to go to bed.

'Tomorrow the three of us will have our first Christmas walk to the Ambrose Rock,' I said.

'You've said that before, or something like it.'

'When?'

'It was our first Christmas in the cottage, and Monty was on the sofa just like Ambrose is now ... and you said that the three of us would have a walk round Minack.'

'And did we?'

'As it happens, we didn't!'

'Why was that?'

'I had made the mistake of giving Monty the turkey giblets at breakfast time ... and he spent the rest of the day sound asleep.'

'You hear that, Ambrose?' I said, and, of course, he was not listening. 'No turkey giblets for you at breakfast time tomorrow!'

TWELVE

Ambrose came on that Christmas Day walk, slowly, peering at a rabbit hole in the hedge, sniffing at a badger track, pretending there was a movement within a patch of flattened bracken, becoming momentarily alert, and when we arrived at the Ambrose Rock he once again jumped up upon it, and began to purr as he did on that first magical walk. He does not always follow us, and sometimes he will stop at the gate and leave us to go on our own. An incident one day gave him such a fright that he left us to go the walk on our own for several weeks.

We were having an amiable walk, nearing the Ambrose Rock, when a dog, a mongrel, suddenly appeared and, without more ado, chased Ambrose into the undergrowth as if he were chasing a rabbit. We did not find Ambrose again for a couple of hours.

The dog was with a middle-aged man, a stranger to us, whom I realised must have followed us through the gate marked Private. Naturally I remonstrated with him, but he replied in a tone that implied that I was at fault. We were to experience such trespasser types from time to time, and I was always constantly amazed by their 'aggro' attitudes.

I once surprised a group of people holding butterfly nets and with trowels for digging up wild plants, and when I told them to get off the land, one of them became so abusive and threatening that Jeannie, watching the situation through field-glasses from the bridge at Minack, hurried to my rescue. She brought a camera with her and she started photographing the offenders, as if for future legal action, while they were being escorted by me from the area. It was funny. She had no film in the camera. It was pretence on her part.

There is, of course, a public path on our land, the Coastal Path, which is under the control of the Countryside Commission, but maintained by the Cornwall County Council. It is, as I have observed before, an admirable path, giving pleasure to many but, recently, it has been causing problems to those responsible for the land through which it passes.

The problems revolve around hikers who decide to camp at the side of the path rather than at an approved camping site. As a result, land beside the path is fouled, tin cans and plastic bottles left in the grass and, in summer, there is the threat from camp fires. The Countryside Commission, however, has now taken steps to warn potential campers that it's illegal to camp.

The section of the Coastal Path on our land runs from the west boundary, which is the low wall where Minack territory begins, to our east boundary at Carn Barges. There is dense undergrowth separating the Coastal Path from the main area of our land and if anyone were to force a way through this undergrowth it could cause serious trouble. The donkeys would be sure to find it and be delighted to do so, and heaven knows how far along the Coastal Path they might go. They would also be in danger. The path between Carn Barges and Lamorna is close to the cliff edge ... so close that a beautiful Dalmatian belonging to a friend of ours, excitedly enjoying itself, fell over the cliff and was killed.

This stretch of Cornish coast is now safe from exploitation, and the inhabitants of the land are safe too. It is an unofficial Nature Reserve. One of the results of our discussions with conservation experts, including those of the Cornwall Naturalists' Trust, was to become even more aware that the inhabitants ... the plant life, the insects, the foxes, badgers, rabbits, butterflies, lizards, even adders ... are the true inhabitants of a wild countryside. The inhabitants of Oliver land, therefore, are now able to lead their natural lives, without snares being set, or the trapping of foxes, and without anyone killing them for fun, or disturbing them with noisy human actions. Such conservation does not necessarily mean total preservation. One has to be sensible. One is defeating one's object if a section of the inhabitants runs riot. After all, had the human race controlled its population explosion, much anguish in the world would have been spared.

When I am walking on our land, when I am sensing the peace which envelops me, when I remember that only the year before we had suddenly learnt that the land was for sale, and that a planning application had been made for a caravan and all the extras that might have resulted ... noise, lack of privacy, dogs chasing Ambrose, bulldozers changing the landscape ... I despair at the thought of such political slogans as 'fair shares for all'. How can there ever possibly be fair shares? The slogan suggests that we all fit into a slot. All of us are beautiful, and clever, and hard-working, and good-tempered, and healthy, and have an equal amount of good luck bestowed upon us. But it is wrong to suggest that such an ideal situation is a mirror of reality.

In our case, Jeannie's and mine, where would we be without the good luck which came to us just at the right time? Supposing we had not walked the path from Lamorna to Carn Barges that summer day and seen Minack cottage empty? Supposing we had been working down the cliff that afternoon when Margaret called and told us that the land on the other side of the valley was for sale? Supposing, supposing ... the lucky ones are the few. The slogan of 'fair shares for all' represents a fraudulent prospectus. In every sphere of life the unlucky ones are the majority.

I know little about our land as yet. I do not yet feel that I belong. I am still observing. I feel more in tune, however, when I have done a few hours' work, like opening up the old bulb meadow with the Condor in January, then picking the old-fashioned daffodils in March. Working the land gives you a strange sense of being respected. It may sound silly, but at all times I feel the land and its inhabitants are the boss. The role of Jeannie and me is to help them preserve their independence from worthy people who believe that the actions of the human race are inviolable.

But dreamers may walk our land; those, young or old, whose worries can be stilled by solitude amongst wild beauty; who can become refreshed by the sense of timelessness, and so free themselves for a while from the complexities of the struggle for personal survival. These complexities seem to me to become ever more complicated when I read and listen to those who pour out words of advice, religious or political, about solving them. I become bewildered, as if lost in a dense verbal forest. I admire the skill of the speakers and writers who can produce such verbosity, and they may create an image that they are leading their followers to a Nirvana, but to me they are only leading them to further confusion. Simplicity, I believe, is what one should seek. Bury the myriad theoretical dogmas which have brought such distress in the past, and strive to achieve simplicity in behaviour towards others, in one's thoughts, in one's daily life.

'The test of religion, the final test of religion, is not religiousness, but Love.'

I recognise the dreamers because they are the vulnerable ones. They come within the category of the insecure, those whom personnel managers describe as non-executive material. They are those who have romantic fantasies and expectations. They are those who will understand without you laboriously having to explain. They are those who, at some moment of their lives, may have failed to accept an opportunity which awaited them, or have been saddened by a hoped-for relationship which did not materialise. They are the sensitive. I am at ease with the dreamers. They are seekers of simplicity. They are at home amongst wild beauty because they find solitude a solace; a moment for peace of mind.

A moment, now and then, is all one can expect. Peace of mind can never be permanent. There is always, in the wings, failure, or anger, or frustration, or financial worry, jostling to destroy it. The peace of mind that I know comes from those moments when suddenly, exultantly, I become aware of the magic around me, aware of mysteries that man-made devices can never explain. I feel free of being a computer number. I am alone with myself. I am part of the magic.

Bluebells proliferate on Oliver land in the spring, and the tiny white flowers of the stitchwort mingle with them, and pink campion too; pink campion much loved by the donkeys. A clump of violets shelter in the shade of a gorse bush ablaze with yellow, the scent of its yellow petals touching me as I pass. An early foxglove stands alone, a sentinel with its deep pink cups, promising a profusion of foxgloves to come. Airship-shaped white clouds are high in the sky above the sea, drifting towards the Lizard, a wren rattles a warning note and, flying up the valley from Minack cliff is a gull, circling the cottage, then settling on the roof. Fascinating to watch because, although at the cottage we see a gull settle, we do not see the route it follows to reach the cottage.

As summer begins there are the white umbrellas of the hawthorn dotted about above the growing bracken and, amidst the bracken and clumps of gorse, birds busy themselves, and a whitethroat, visitor from North Africa, will suddenly spiral upwards twittering its song. Swallows are flying in from the west. A buzzard, high above the Q.E.2 field, is being chivied by a raven; a fisherman in his crabber is pulling in his pots, there is a shadow on the grass in front of me as a cloud passes the sun, and the path to the Ambrose Rock is spattered with violets and celandines.

I lean against the Ambrose Rock, Carn Barges a little to my left, the cottage in the distance to my right, and I remember the first time we saw Minack:

'There was never any doubt in either of our minds. The small grey cottage a mile away, squat in the lonely landscape, surrounded by trees and edged into the side of a hill, became as if by magic the present and the future. It was as if a magician beside this ancient Carn had cast a spell upon us, so that we would touch the future as we could, at that moment, touch the Carn. There, in the distance, we could see our figures moving about our daily tasks, a thousand, thousand figures criss-crossing the untamed land, dissolving into each other, leaving a mist of excitment of our times to come.'

As I lean against the Ambrose Rock, it is soothing to remember that moment.

Monty was with us then.

179

His double is with us today.
A sense of timelessness.

THE HEARTWARMING TRUE STORY
OF A VERY SPECIAL DOG
AND HER VERY SPECIAL OWNER

SHEILA HOCKEN

EMMA V.I.P.

(Illus)

Everyone knows the inspiring story of Sheila Hocken and
her wonderful guide-dog Emma, and of the miracle
operation which enabled her to see for the first time in her
life.

Now, Sheila describes her life since the incredible moment
when she opened her eyes and saw the beautiful world we
all take for granted. With freshness and humour, Sheila
tells how each day brought new joys, new challenges and
new surprises.

Emma's life, too, has undergone dramatic changes. She was
no longer needed as a guide-dog but her retirement has
been far from idle. She is now a celebrity and receives her
own fan mail; she has made several television appearances;
she was Personality Dog of the Year at Crufts and is greeted
in the street more often than Sheila is.

'Writing simply, with innate ability to externalise thought,
feeling, experience, she again achieves a lovable intimacy'
Daily Telegraph

AUTOBIOGRAPHY   0 7221 4601 9   £1.25

Also by Sheila Hocken in Sphere Books:
EMMA AND I

THE COUNTRY DIARY OF AN EDWARDIAN LADY

Edith Holden

The new pocket edition of Edith Holden's bestselling **THE COUNTRY DIARY OF AN EDWARDIAN LADY** has all the charm and natural beauty of the first edition. This beautiful book not only makes an ideal gift, but is also now compact enough to take on country rambles so that you too can enjoy nature as the author herself did at the height of the Edwardian era.

AUTOBIOGRAPHY   0 7221 0580 0   £4.50

WHALE

JEREMY LUCAS

A classic story of the sea, WHALE tells of the love, loyalty and life of Sabre, a killer whale.

'We believe in Sabre, the killer whale whose fortunes we follow. Jeremy Lucas' respect for the species is infectious. There are some awe-inspiring descriptions of the way these intelligent animals care for each other, how they comfort the wounded and dying, protect the cows and calves . . . this is a fascinating piece of work.'
Daily Telegraph

'Mr Lucas' whales are capable of grief, clemency, conscientious leadership; they can harbour old grudges, adopt orphans and extend a helping fin in trouble. He knows his whales, and brings a lyrical determination to the *life-and-death dance of creation.'*
Observer

'This excellent first novel is moving, original and *enlightening. It ought to become a classic of its kind.'*
New Statesman

GENERAL FICTION   0 7221 5640 5   £1.75

A selection of bestsellers from SPHERE

FICTION

DEEP SIX	Clive Cussler	£2.25 ☐
MILLENNIUM	John Varley	£1.99 ☐
SMART WOMEN	Judy Blume	£2.25 ☐
INHERITORS OF THE STORM	Victor Sondheim	£2.95 ☐
HEADLINES	Bernard Weinraub	£2.75 ☐

FILM & TV TIE-INS

THE RIVER	Steven Bauer	£1.95 ☐
WATER	Gordon McGill	£1.75 ☐
THE DUNE STORYBOOK	Joan D. Vinge	£2.50 ☐
NO-ONE KNOWS WHERE		
GOBO GOES	Mark Saltzman	£1.50 ☐
BOOBER FRAGGLE'S CELERY		
SOUFFLÉ	Louise Gikow	£1.50 ☐

NON-FICTION

PAUL ERDMAN'S MONEY		
GUIDE	Paul Erdman	£2.95 ☐
THE 1985 FAMILY WELCOME GUIDE		
	Jill Foster and Malcolm Hamer	£3.95 ☐
THE OXFORD CHILDREN'S DICTIONARY		
	John Weston and Alan Spooner	£3.25 ☐
THE *WOMAN* BOOK OF LOVE AND SEX		
	Deidre Sanders	£1.95 ☐
INTO THE REMOTE PLACES	Ian Hibell with	
	Clinton Trowbridge	£2.95 ☐

All Sphere books are available at your local bookshop or newsagent, or can be ordered direct from the publisher. Just tick the titles you want and fill in the form below.

Name_____

Address_____

_____

Write to Sphere Books, Cash Sales Department, P.O. Box 11, Falmouth, Cornwall TR10 9EN

Please enclose cheque or postal order to the value of the cover price plus:

UK: 55p for the first book, 22p for the second book and 14p per copy for each additional book ordered to a maximum charge of £1.75.

OVERSEAS: £1.00 for the first book and 25p per copy for each additional book.

BFPO & EIRE: 55p for the first book, 22p for the second book plus 14p per copy for the next 7 books, thereafter 8p per book.

Sphere Books reserve the right to show new retail prices on covers which may differ from those previously advertised in the text or elsewhere, and to increase postal rates in accordance with the PO.